Living Privately in Public: Social Media and Responsibility

By

Students and Alumni

of

Texas Lutheran University

CONTENTS

ACKNOWLEDGMENTS

Thank you to Daniel Solove, Steven Rambam and Dr. Sherry Turkle, the speakers whose work inspired and provoked discussion among Texas Lutheran University's students, faculty, and staff. Thanks also to the Krost Symposium planning committee for 2011: Carolyn Turner, Robin Bisha, Sam Hijazi, and Steven Vrooman.

1 Looking to Meet New Friends: Reactions to Sex and Race on Craigslist

By

Amber Mellon, Melissa Fike, Zoila Garcia, Canaan Hoffmann, Kyle Leihsing, and Tiffiny Sia, Ph.D.

Special Acknowledgements to all of the confederates who provided their photos: Kyle McNally, Shantik Taylor, Jose Rincon, and Tamara Schmoekel. Also, thank you to Morgan Hale for data analysis on Craigslist study 1. We would also like to thank Joshua Haby for providing data collection and support in Nebraska.

Abstract

The Internet has become the new outlet for meeting new people and so people are now more willing to give out personal information than ever before. This series of studies utilized Craigslist and focused on how people responded to ads of differing ethnicity and sex. Although each of these studies looked at responses to ethnicities/sex, there were different primary focuses. Study 1 focused on ethnicity and responses to level of provocativeness of confederate photos and scripts. Study 2 focused primarily on responses to confederates posting a poem rejecting their stereotype. Study 3 focused on how minorities were treated differently in a diverse population versus in Texas and Nebraska. The first study showed significance in number of photos received with females having received more photos than males. Provocative ads received significantly more aggression than the neutral ads. The females received more explicit language than the males. The White male received significantly more replies than the Black male while the Black female received more responses than White female. In Study 2 the White male received significantly more responses and than the Hispanic male. Overall, Hispanics were flirted with more than Whites. Study 3 showed the Hispanic female received more responses in Texas than in Nebraska. There was also significance found for level of flirtatiousness and friendliness with the Black female having received more than the White and Hispanic females. Additionally, those who responded to the Black female had a mean age higher than the mean age of respondents to the White and Hispanic females.

Key Words: Social Media, Craigslist, Ethnicity, Midwest, South, Aggression, Flirtatiousness

Every academic year, Texas Lutheran University hosts the Krost Symposium. The symposium has a theme to enlighten to students more on a specific topic. The Fall 2011 topic was "Living Privately in Public." Speakers were flown in to teach the students how much social media has been slowly integrated into our society and people are not taking the necessary precautions. In today's current society, the Internet has become a new outlet for meeting new people. It seems that it is now acceptable to meet people online without having to give your real name and information. The following studies were conducted on the Craigslist social media website (Hoffmann et. al, 2011, Garcia et. al, 2011, Fike, Pfenninger, Haby, and Sia, 2011). Though each study followed the same overall theme of responses towards ethnicity and sex, each had a different primary focus.

The first Craigslist study was performed in Dallas, Texas, and looked at ethnicity (white and black) and responses to level of provocativeness. Previous research has suggested that Internet communities can become pathological. (Durkin et al., 2006). People are using the Internet and adding certain risks in meeting people. Some people assume that since it is through the Internet that it is acceptable to take risks not otherwise taken when meeting someone in person, e.g. giving unseen strangers' photos, addresses, phone numbers, personal preferences, etc. Recent news reports have suggested that Craigslist is easily subverted to non benign uses like prostitution, identity theft, and cyber bullying. Previous research has suggested that social barriers are different online (i.e. sexist harassment is more tolerated; Serafino, Haby, Sia, Czuchry, 2010).

Our first study examined if people of different races are likely to receive more sexual harassment, aggression, explicit language, propositions, and personal information like photos, phone numbers, addresses, etc.

The second Craigslist study looked at how individuals responded to confederates who provided poems breaking away from their ethnic and gender stereotypes. In a gender studies class, a female student created a poster with a photo. The poem was talking about not wanting to be defined as a Hispanic female. The poster was defaced with accusations of being hostile towards males despite never mentioning males. We wanted to replicate and investigate whether poems of other races and sexes would receive the same types of hostility. Stereotypes for both a given race and sex role (Hispanic /white and male/ female) are prolific in society (Lyson, 1986). The third Craigslist study examines the treatment of women on the "platonic" section of Craigslist in the Midwest (Nebraska) and the South (Texas). Our first study centered in Texas showed that females received more propositions and hostility on 'women-seeking-men' section of Craigslist (Hoffmann, et al., 2011). The third study was designed to examine how minorities were treated differently in a diverse, predominately urban population versus a less diverse, predominately rural population using Texas and Nebraska.

Study 1: Reactions to sex, race, and provocativeness of the ad

Method

Respondents

There were 222 participants, 58 females and 162 males, which responded to the Craigslist ads (see table 1 for details). We believe we had 28% white, 18% black, 7% Hispanic 6% other, and 40% unknown. It is likely that we misidentified ethnicity since we were going by photo or name less that 50% of the time respondents gave us their ethnicity. Because of this ambiguity we didn't feel comfortable doing additional analysis on ethnicity. We could not ask the respondents for ethnicity without jeopardizing the privacy of our confederates.

Table 1. Numbers of males and females by condition

		Sex			Total
		Male	Female	Unknown	
Confederate	WF	41	0	0	41
	BF	111	1	0	112
	WM	2	35	1	38
	BM	7	22	1	30
Total		161	58	2	221

Materials

Photos: Four confederates were recruited to represent white and black, male and female college aged people. The age range for the confederates was 20-25. Ironically, the oldest confederate, our white female, was kicked off the site twice for looking under age. None of the other confederate's photos were tagged for removal on Craigslist. Names used with the ads were pseudonyms to protect the privacy of the confederates. All four confederates gave permission for their photos to be posted in Dallas, Texas.

Figure 1. Confederate photos (Conservative)

| "Adam"- Black male | "Danielle"- White female | "Trisha"- Black female | "Kyle"- White male |

Advertisement Scripts: Basic scripts that were in line with what was seen on Craigslist were created. One was seen as casual and the other was seen as provocative (See figure 2 for examples).

Figure 2. Advertisement Scripts

Casual Ads:

"Hey I'm(Insert Name Here), I'm (Insert Age here) and new to the area. I'm looking to meet new friends around the area, and thought it would be a good idea to start here. I'll be taking responses to the ad as long as it is posted, can't wait to meet some friendly and fun people."

Provocative Ads:

"Hey I'm (Insert Name Here), looking to meet some sexy guys/girls. I'm (Insert Age Here) and hot to meet you. If you're wanting the same as me and "I know you are," feel free to respond to the ad as long as it is up. Can't wait to meet you sexy men/women so the faster you respond the better."

Checklist: A checklist was used to document responses and included Likert scales for Aggression, Friendliness, and Flirtatiousness (See figure 3 for example).

Figure 3. Participant Observation Checklist

```
                    Participant Observation Checklist
Craig's list personal ad's:      Women seeking Men      Men seeking Women
Sex of respondent:       Male  Female
Approximate Race of respondent:( self identified or in photo)
White                 Black                 Hispanic              Other
Aggression level in message:
1          2          3          4          5
Friendly                       Demeaning
Friendliness level in message:
1          2          3          4          5
Not at all                               Very
Flirtatiousness level in message:
1          2          3          4          5
Not at all                               Very
Explicit language: (e.g. swear words, sexual propositions, & deviant language)
Photo given: Yes No
Photo: (Coded for explicitness)
```

Results

A Chi Square analysis showed significant difference for the white male confederate and the black female confederate, $\underline{X}^2$ (1) =18, $p < .01$. The white male confederate received more than expected replies while the black male confederate received less than expected replies. The black female confederate received more than expected replies while the white female confederate less than expected replies (See Figure 4).

Figure 4. Number of Responses to Posted Ad

	Male	Female
White	38	41
Black	30	112

An ANOVA with confederate and neutral/provocative of ad as independent variable was run with photos as dependent variable. There was a significant main effect for confederates such that the African American female (65%) and white female (85%) received photos more often than the males (8%), $F(3, 212) = 18.74$, $\eta^2 = 0.209$, $p \leq .05$. See Table 2 below for means.

Table 2. Photos received by confederates

	White Female Ad		Black Female Ad		White Male Ad		Black Male Ad		Total	
	Mean (SD)		Mean (SD)		Mean (SD)		Mean (SD)		Mean (SD)	
Casual	.85 (.367)	n=13	.65 (.485)	n=13	.08 (.277)	n=13	.08 (.277)	n=26	.46 (.502)	n=65
Provocative	.46 (.508)	n=28	.66 (.477)	n=85	.16 (.477))	n=25	.24 (.437)	n=17	.24 (.437)	n=155

An ANOVA with confederate and neutral/provocative of ad as independent variable was run with aggressiveness as dependent variable. There was a significant main effect for neutral/provocative ads with provocative ads receiving more aggression than neutral ads. $F(1, 212) = 4.41$, $\eta^2 = 0.020$, $p \leq .05$. White males received significantly more aggression than any other confederate. $F(3, 212) = 10.71$, $\eta^2 = 0.131$, $p \leq .05$. Female respondents claimed that the White male confederate was a predator or questioned his orientation. They told him that he was a danger to women everywhere. In contrast, the black male confederate was offered Dallas Mavericks tickets in exchange for a home visit, apparently without much concern about him being dangerous.

Table 3. Mean aggressiveness towards confederate's ads

	White Female Ad		Black Female Ad		White Male Ad		Black Male Ad		Total	
	Mean (SD)		Mean (SD)		Mean (SD)		Mean (SD)		Mean (SD)	
Casual	2.85(1.57)	n=13	2.31 (1.75)	n=13	1.46(1.26)	n=13	1.38(1.02)	n=26	1.88(1.43)	n=65
Provocative	1.68 (9.38)	n=28	1.33 (.851)	n=85	2.24(1.589)	n=25	1.24(.831)	n=17	1.53(1.071)	n=155

An ANOVA with confederate and neutral/provocative of ad as independent variable was run with explicit language as dependent variable. There was significant main effect for casual/provocative ad such that provocatives received more explicit language than non-provocative ad. $F(1, 212) = 5.78$, $\square^2 = 0.026$ $p \leq .05$. There was a main effect for confederate that females received more explicit language than males. $F(3, 212) = 2.71$, $\square^2 = 0.037$, $p \leq .05$. For example, the black female confederate was shown pictures of a male with a former lover, and the male told the black confederate that could be her.

Table 4. Mean explicit language used

	White Female Ad		Black Female Ad		White Male Ad		Black Male Ad		Total	
	Mean (SD)		Mean (SD)		Mean (SD)		Mean (SD)		Mean (SD)	
Casual	.46(.776)	n=13	.35 (.562)	n=13	.00(0.00)	n=13	.23 (.599)	n=26	.28 (.573)	n=65
Provocative	.04(.189)	n=28	.18(.413)	n=85	.04(.200)	n=25	.12(.485)	n=17	.12(.366)	n=155

Discussion

Males were more willing to take risks in sending photos than females. The females wanted more proof that the ads were real before continuing the interaction. The more provocative ads triggered more aggression. The white male had their sexuality questioned or was accused of being a predator. Respondents may have been more politically correct with black confederates. Although our provocative ads were not explicit, they triggered more explicit language than the neutral ad. Females were exposed to more explicit materials than the male confederates. Females received more propositions and descriptions of desired activities.

Study 2: Reactions to breaking stereotypes of sex and race

This second study included a poem that addressed the racial stereotypical roles of ethnicity and gender and there were no provocative ads. Hispanic confederates were recruited instead of Black confederates. The ads were posted in six different Texas cities. We wanted to replicated and explore the aggression the Hispanic female had seen with her poster.

Methods

Respondents

There were 409 respondents, 368 males and 41 females, which responded to the Craigslist ads (see table 5 for details).

Table 5. Number of males and females by condition

	Male	Female	Total
Total participants	306	41	409
White male ad	1	23	24
Hispanic female ad	306	2	308
Hispanic male ad	0	15	15
White female ad	61	1	62

Materials

Photos: There were four confederates recruited to represent Hispanic and white, male and female college aged people. Names used with the ads were pseudonyms to protect the privacy of the confederates. All four confederates gave permission for their photos to be posted in 6 different Texas cities.

Figure 5: Confederate photos

"Maria" Hispanic female   "Sarah"- white female   "Jose" – Hispanic male   "James" – white male

Figure 6: Confederates' Poems

Hispanic female poem	Hispanic male poem
I am a Woman I am a woman… In a society that doesn't accept my culture. In a culture that judges us by our traditions. And a woman isn't a woman unless she's pure. So I am divided between what I should be and what I want I want to be. I am a woman that wants to be accepted by society, And at the same time by my culture, Yet I don't want to be defined by my culture or society. So I am what I decided to be at the end of the day. I am a woman with no boundaries I am a woman with no fears, And a woman with desires So whatever they call me at the end of the day doesn't really matter. Because at the end of the day I am a woman that looks like no other A woman that acts likes no other. So define me, define me not!	I am a Man I am a man… In a society that doesn't accept my culture. In a culture that judges us by our traditions. And a man isn't a man unless he has respect So I am divided between what I should be and what I want to be. I am a man that wants to be accepted by society, And at the same time by my culture, Yet I don't want to be defined by my culture or society. So I am what I decide to be at the end of the day. I am a man with no boundaries I am a man with no fears, And a man with compassion and humility So whatever they call me at the end of the day doesn't really matter. Because at the end of the day I am a man that looks like no other A man that acts like no other So define me, define me not!

White female poem	White male poem
I am Beauty Myth	I am the Blues
I am a woman ...	I am the blues...
In a society that doesn't accept my flaws ,	I am white and male ,
Flaws that not only define my beauty and intelligence, but my worth	Competitive and strong.
If I do not maintain the youthful image of womanly perfection	I am the blues.
Not only is my beauty diminished, but also my worth.	So am I less?
I am divided between what I should be and what I want to be	Because I am not from an oppressed culture
I am a woman that wants to be admired by society	Because I don't come from a people once oppressed?
And at the same time admired for who I am,	Yet I am what I decide to be at the end of the day
Yet I don't want to be defined by my flaws or society.	I am the blues.
At the end of the day I am what I am determined to be.	The blues is life...
I am a woman of worth with no boundaries.	Do none of these apply?
I am a woman of intelligence with no fears.	If my skin is white,
Whoever chooses to label me and assign value does so in vain	Define me, define me as you will
Because I am a woman that looks like no other	That's your own proverbial pill
And acts like no other	Because in my veins I am the blues.
So define me, define me not!	So define me, define me not!

Checklist: The original checklist was modified to include racial language used by respondents. Explicit language was made more detailed by categorizing by type of explicit language. Racial slurs would be words like the "N word." Sexist words would be "slut," "whore." Religious language would be "Hell." Profanity was the "F" word and fecal matter. A checklist was used to document responses and included Likert scales for Aggression, Friendliness, and Flirtatiousness (See figure 6 for example).

Figure 7: Participant Observation Checklist

Participant Observation Checklist

Sex of respondent: Male   Female

Approximate Race of respondent: (self identified or in photo)

White   Black   Hispanic Asia   Middle Eastern   Other

Racial Language Used: (e.g. White, Black and Hispanic) List words

Explicit Language: (circle all that apply)

racial slurs   sexist terms   religious language   profanity

Photo: (Coded for number received and deviance of photo)

Yes   No

Aggression level in message:

Procedures

For this experiment photos and poems were posted in six Texas cities: McAllen, Abilene, San Antonio, Austin, Corpus Christi, and Laredo. The ads were posted in six cities to get a broad range of participants around Texas. The posting in Corpus Christi and Laredo did not receive any responses.

Results

A Chi Square analysis showed significant differences on numbers of responses with race and sex as the independent variables, $\chi^2 (1) = 42.58$, $p < .05$. The white male received more responses than expected compared to the Hispanic male who received less than expected.

Figure 8. Number of Responses to Posted Ad

	Male	Female
White	24	63
Hispanic	7	309

A MANOVA was run with sex and ethnicity as the independent variable and flirtatiousness and friendliness as the dependent variables. A significant interaction was found for flirtatiousness, $F (1,406) = 10.412$, $\eta^2 = 0.025$ $p \leq .05$. The white male received more flirtatiousness than Hispanic male, while the Hispanic female received more flirtatiousness than the white female. The white female confederate was told that she was too beautiful to have problems, that her problems could not possibly be real.

Table 6. Mean (SD) Friendliness and Flirtatiousness based on ethnicity and sex

Friendliness	Male	Female
White	3.38 (1.408) n=24	2.92 (1.076) n=62
Hispanic	2.93 (1.408) n= 15	3.08 (.814) n= 309

Flirtatiousness		
White	2.79 (1.615) n= 24	1.65 (1.073) n=62
Hispanic	2.07 (1.033) n=15	1.90 (.693) n= 309

The second MANOVA used racial language, sexist language, religious language and profanity for dependent variables. A significant interaction was found on profanity, F (1,406) =6.438, η^2 =0.016 $p\leq$ .05. The white male received more profanity than the Hispanic male, while females received none. The white male confederate had females propositioning him for sexual activities.

Discussion

Females were more flirtatious with white males than Hispanic males. Since the white male is breaking his stereotype, are females breaking their sex role stereotype by pursuing him? Males were more flirtatious with the Hispanic female than the white female. Males may have liked the atypical Hispanic female expressed in the poem. The white male received more profanity than the Hispanic male while the females received no profanity. Are people more excepting of minorities by wanting to break out of a stereotypical role than majorities?

We did not replicate the hostility initially shown in the poster. The defacement of the poster may have been due to the fairly anonymous responses. Although Craigslist is anonymous, our respondents expected to engage in a conversation with authors of the poem and were relatively friendly. In the Craigslist paradigm, hostility might be indicated by a lack of response rather than slurs in the content of messages.

Study 3: Comparison of reactions to females on Craigslist.

This third Craigslist study differs from the other two in that it posted in two different states; one culturally diverse (Texas) and the other predominantly white (Nebraska). It was supposed to look at male and female differences, but our males received almost no responses in Nebraska. In order to do analysis, the results focused exclusively at the treatment of women of three different ethnic groups as compared to the other studies that used only two. This study also used a neutral ad similar to Study 1.

Method

Respondents

There were 525 respondents ranging from ages 18-49. 321 people out of 525 reported their race (Table 9).

Table 7. Respondents by ethnicity

Respondent ethnicity	# of responses	% of total responses	% of responses who reported ethnicity
White	105	20%	32.7%
Black	62	11.8%	19.3%
Hispanic	131	25%	40.8%
Asian	9	1.7%	2.8%
Middle Eastern	9	1.7%	2.8%
Other	5	1%	1.6%
Did not report race	204	38.9%	N/A

Materials

Scripts: Basic scripts were constructed following a basic template (see Figure 9) that were in line with what was seen on the platonic section of the Craigslist personal ads.

Figure 9. Confederates' script

"Hey I'm (INSERT CONFEDERATE NAME HERE) I'm 22 years old and just moved to the area. I'm looking to meet new friends around here, and thought this would be a good place to start. I'll be taking responses to the ad as long as it is posted, can't wait to meet some friendly and fun people!"

Photos: Six confederates were recruited to represent White; Hispanic, and Black, male and female college aged people. The age range for the confederates was 20-22 (see Table 7). A major problem occurred when the female confederates (initially, listed at 22 years old) were flagged multiple times for removal, some days up to three times in one day. Interestingly the white female was flagged the most and the black female was flagged the least. Interestingly, once our female reduced her age by two years (20 years old) she was flagged less. The white female also received an offer to acquire a "sugar daddy."

Figure 10. Confederates' photos

| "Stephanie" | "Latisha" | "Maria" |
| "Nick"* NE n=0 | "Jamal"* NE n=3 | "Juan"* NE n=0 |

Procedures

The ads were posted using the Dallas, Texas Craigslist, the Houston, Texas Craigslist, and the Lincoln, Nebraska Craigslist. Regional differences between Nebraska and Texas are: Rural (NE 41% vs. TX 12%), White (NE 82% vs. TX 45%), and Hispanic (NE 9% vs. TX 37%), and Black (NE 5% vs. TX 12%). The ads were posted in two different Texas cities due to the fact that some of the other cities we had tried to post in would not show our ads even if it said they were online so in order to assure success we posted in two cities. Lincoln, Nebraska did not have this problem. Nebraska was chosen as the less diverse state instead of any other state because the researchers were collaborating with a student at the University of Nebraska, Lincoln and one of the experimenters is originally from Nebraska and so she knew what the area was like. In each of the cities the ads were posted under the "Strictly Platonic" heading of the personal advertisement section.

The ads were each posted in their respective cities on weeknights. We did not post on weekends to keep consistency as to which type of people would be on craigslist at the time of posting. Three were posted in each city at a time in order to avoid suspicion due to the similarities of the advertisements. On the first posting for each study the White male, Black female, and Hispanic male were posted. On the second posting for each study the White female, Black male and Hispanic female were posted. Each of the ads was to be left up for 48 hours but there were complications. Since our female confederates kept getting flagged and removed multiple times in the 48 hour period we had to correct for time lost by reposting the advertisements. Our males received little to no posts each in each city and so they were left up indefinitely in order to gain responses but they never reached the number of responses necessary for analysis.

Results

A chi-squared analysis revealed a significant difference. $\underline{X}^2(1) = 17.33$, p<.05. HFC received more than expected responses in Texas and less in Nebraska, perhaps due to a more diverse population and more familiarity with the Hispanic race.

Table 8. Chi Square Location x Confederate Race

	White female	Hispanic female	Black female
Nebraska	33	9	28
Texas	158	174	123

A MANOVA was conducted with confederate race and location as IVs and response flirtatiousness (high vs. low) and friendliness (high vs. low) as DVs. There was a multivariate effect. $\underline{F}(4, 1034)= 3.89$, $p<.05$. Black Female Confederates received significantly higher flirtatious ($\underline{F}[2,518]=3.62$, $p<.05$) and friendly ($\underline{F}[2,518]= 5.20$, $p<.05$) responses than the White Female Confederate or Hispanic Female Confederate. The black female even received propositions of an exchange of money for sexual behaviors.

Table 9. Mean Flirtatiousness and Friendliness x Race of Confederate

	Count	Mean flirtatiousness (SD)	Mean Friendliness (SD)
White female	191	1.644 (8.297)	2.97 (8.297)
Hispanic female	183	1.530 (8.477)	3.00 (8.477)
Black female	150	2.106 (9.363)	3.34 (9.363)

The main effect for location and flirtatiousness approached significance. Nebraskans (M=1.92) were more flirtatious than Texans (M=1.59), a finding of interest due to the disparate population composition. This could be indicative of wanting something outside the norm.

Table 10. Mean Flirtatiousness x Location

	Count	Mean	SD
Nebraska	70	1.594	(.1370)
Texas	454	1.927	(5.382)

ANOVAs were run with Confederate Race and Location as IVs. The first ANOVA's dependent variable was ethnicity of respondents. A main effect was found for Location, $F(1,315)= 2.30$, $p<.05$, $\square^2 = .0072$. Respondents were more diverse in Texas (M=2.35) than Nebraska (M=1.23).

Table 11. Race x Location

	Count	Mean	SD
Nebraska	27	1.229	(.207)
Texas	294	2.350	(6.297)

The second ANOVA's dependent variable is Respondent Age. A main effect for Respondent Race was found, with Respondents to Black Female Confederate (M=30.68) significantly older than White Female Confederate (M=26.91) and HFC (M=25.34), $F(2,162)=3.60$, $p<.05$, $\square^2= .043$.

Table 12. Age of Respondents x Race of Confederate

	n	Mean	SD
White female	71	27 yrs old	.684
Hispanic female	57	25 yrs old	.673
Black female	40	37 years old	.911

Discussion

Nebraskans showed less interest in Hispanics which raises a question on whether Nebraskans have a stronger stereotype of Hispanics due to unfamiliarity, or potentially as a product of current anti immigration media.

The responses to the black female were friendlier, more flirtatious, and from an older population when compared to the responses to the other females. This could be indicative of Black females being viewed as highly sexualized, fitting the Black Jezebel stereotype (Donovan, 2009). Our findings show that Black females will receive more attention, but some of that attention may be unwanted (e.g. exhibitionistic photos). We did not find the level of hostility and aggression that previous research (Hoffmann et al, 2011) had found, probably because we posted under platonic rather than dating. It would have been interesting to go more in depth by responding to some of the ads, but, out of concern for the safety of the confederates this was not allowed in the procedure.

Conclusions

There were consistencies seen in some of the studies. For instance in studies one and two, the white males received the most aggressive responses to their ads. Then in studies two and three the minority females received more flirtatious and friendly responses compared to the White females. Perhaps this is due to the stereotype of minority females. One way to examine this is to post stereotypical vs. non-stereotypical photos of the confederates and see if respondents flirted more with the stereotypical than the non-stereotypical. There was an inconsistency for the third study in that we did not see any aggression. This could be due to the fact that most of the aggressions for those studies were aimed at the white male, and instead of aggressiveness the males were just ignored. Perhaps, the aggression was increased by the provocativeness of the first photo and the poem for the second.

One extension of the second study could include black confederates and more controversial poems versus the tamer, already existing poems. A control should also be added to the second study to examine what kind of effects the poems are having on the responders.

There did seem to be a wide diversity of responses on-line and responses are almost instantaneous. Our white female confederate received 33 responses in 27 minutes. It should be noticed that many of the respondents were friendly concerned and even warned confederates about being careful on-line. There was some, but not a lot of solicitation, exhibitionism, and except for the white male no instances of threats or bullying. Probably more could be elicited by use of different photos or ads (e.g. confederates wearing t-shirts with political slogans). However, if this line of research were pursued, it is important for the confederates to have independent coders do the checklist, because some of the responses could be hurtful. There was definite dichotomy between responses that would make a person uncomfortable and responses that seemed genuine and interesting.

References

Blingh, M. C., Schleltofer, M. M., Casad, B. J., & Gaffiney, A. M. (2012). Competent enough, but would you

vote for her? Gender stereotypes and media influences on perception of women politicians. *Journal of*

Applied Social Psychology, *42*(3), 560-597.

Durkin, Keith, Forsyth, Craig, Quinn, & James. (2006). Pathological Internet Communities: A new

Direction for Sexual deviance research in a new post modern era. *Social Spectrum*, *26*(6), 595-606.

Evans, A. B., Copping, K. E., Rowley, S. J., & Kurtx-Costes, B. (2011). Academic Self- Concept in Black Adolescents: Do Race and Gender Stereotypes Matter? *Self & Identity, 10*(2), 263-277.

Kliuchko, I. (n.d.). Gender Stereotyping in Studying Pressing Social Problems. *Russian Social Science Review.*

Lopez-Zafra, E., & Garcia- Retamero, R. (2012). Do Gender Stereotypes Change? The dynamic of gender Stereotypes in Spain. *Journal of Gender Studies, 21*(2), 169-183.

Serafino, A. B., Haby, J., Sia, T. L., & Czuchry, M. L. (2012). *Wanna Cyber? The effect of perceived gender interactions within chat rooms.* Dallas, TX: Southwester Psychological Association Conference.

Sharpiro, T., & Amy, W. (2012). The Role of Stereotype Treats in Undermining Girls and Women's Performance and interest in STEM Field. *Sex Roles, 66*(3/), 175-183.

2 Wanna Cyber: A Rose by Any Other Name Will Always Get More Attention Than a Frank

By

Kyle A. Leihsing, Melissa L. Fike, Amber M. Mellon & Tiffiny L.Sia, Ph.D.

Special Acknowledgements: Andrew B. Serafino for the creation of this paradigm, Joshua A. Haby, without whom, none of this would have been possible, and Caleb Hoffmann for running trials when no one else was available.

The Internet provides an important venue for interpersonal communication, although potentially at an interpersonal and personal cost (Kraut et al., 1998). Each year Texas Lutheran University Hosts the Krost Symposium. The topic for 2011 focused on social media and how the sharing of personal information on the Internet has brought up many questions of concern. Namely, how much is too much information and how much personal information is demanded in a Chat Room setting. Although prior work suggested that the presumed sex of chat room participants does not affect the type of interaction occurring in chat rooms (Rollman, Krug, & Parente, 2000), our research conducted a more extensive investigation on how males and females are treated differently in online Chat Rooms and whether or not these online communities breed healthy social interactions or if it is a pathological outlet for individuals to air their unspoken desires. Three Studies were run investigating three ways of differentiating oneself by Screen Name in a Chat Room; strictly by sex (Male vs. Female), by varying degrees of attractiveness of Screen Names (Mertyle vs. Brandi), and by different types of interest (Miss Artist vs. Mistress of Pain).

Study 1: Obviously Male or Female vs. Androgynous Screen Names

Methods

Materials

Chat Rooms: For uniformity, both chat rooms were selected from a single host site (http://www.chat-avenue.com) that contained many different types of chat rooms. Our study utilized two of those chat rooms: "Adult Chat" and "Singles Chat".

The sites were not designated as sex chat rooms, but did contain adult material (18 yrs +). The main purpose of the Chat Rooms appeared to be the pursuit of a potential partner rather than just conversation. An equal number of counter-balanced trials were run in each chat room.

Screen Names: Using the browser-based Chat Rooms, confederates entered using different types of screen names based on current naming trends (Obviously Male, Obviously Female, Androgynous Male, and Androgynous Female). The names are listed below in Table 1.

Table 1: Sample Male/Female/Androgynous Screen Names Used

Male Screen Names	Female Screen Names	Androgynous Male Screen Names	Androgynous Female Screen Names
Michael	Brittney	Bailey	Bailey
Brandon	Megan	Cameron	Cameron
Josh	Kayla	Pat	Pat
Scott	Katie	Drew	Drew
Andrew	Emily	Lee	Mel
David	Liz	Taylor	Devon
James	Stephanie	Alex	Adrian

Procedures

There were 9 trials with the Male Screen Names, 11 trials with the Female Screen Names, 10 trials with the Male Androgynous Screen names, and 11 trials with the Female Androgynous Screen names. The trials consisted of chatting with the first person to send a private message request. The confederates adhered to a script to establish themselves in the Chat Room. Confederates responded neutrally or agreed with whatever the respondent talk about.

Confederates did not make suggestive remarks. If a proposition was received, confederates would politely disengage from the conversation (Table 2).

Table 2: Script for Trials

The confederate logged into a chat room to see if anyone would make contact. ....0-1 minute	
If not contacted, confederate would enter a comment in to the chat room such as "hi room," and see if anyone would make contact. ....1-2 minutes	
If not contacted, confederate would prompt the room with "hey, does anyone want to chat?" and continue to record for any responses. ....2-3 minutes	
If not contacted, confederate would prompt with age/sex of confederate and once again ask the room if anyone wanted to chat. ....3-4 minutes	
At the fourth minute, confederate would repeat the age/sex of confederate and then ask the room if anyone wanted to "cyber.." ....4-5 minutes	

Note: Contact was operationally defined as any private message from anyone in the chat room.

Trials ended if a) the confederate was propositioned or b) 5 minutes had elapsed, whichever came first. During the conversation with the respondent, confederates measured the amount of time until the private message request, if any were received. If contact was made, confederates continued the conversation. The amount of time until the proposition, if received, was also recorded. All respondents that contacted the confederate had a different screen name, and are assumed to be separate individuals.

Results

The confederate was propositioned for cyber sex 9 times out of 41 trials. Of those trials our confederates received 3 cyber propositions for obviously male names, 3 cyber propositions for obviously female names, 3 cyber propositions for androgynous female names, and no cyber propositions for androgynous male names. Two of the propositions the Male Screen Name received were by males who stated they were heterosexual, but wanted to have cyber sex with the male confederate. The third proposition for the Male Screen Name was from a homosexual male.

A MANOVA with Independent Variables (IV) of Male/Female/Androgynous Screen Names and Dependent Variables (DV) of Time Until First Response and Time Until Proposition was run. No significant differences were found for Time Until Proposition, however a Multivariate Main Effects for Sex was found, $F(2,36) = 15.44$, $p < 0.05$. There was also a Significant Multivariate Interaction, $F(2,36) = 6.12$, $p < 0.05$. There was only significant Univariate effects for time until first response for Sex, $F(1,37) = 29.25$, $p < 0.05$, and Interaction, $F(1,37) = 12.58$, $p < 0.05$. This showed that screen names that are clearly female elicit private messages from males more quickly than do other screen names. Androgynous screen names only elicited quicker responses when it became clear that the individual was a female (Figure 1)

Figure 1: Time Until First Response in Seconds

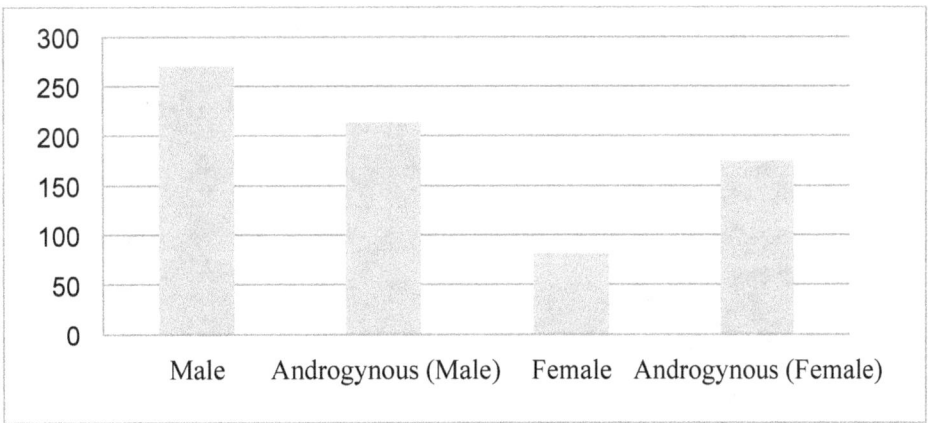

Discussion

Study 1 found that names that were clearly female elicited male responses more quickly than did other names. Only when it became clear that an androgynous name belongs to a female did it elicit a response more quickly. The traditional sex role of men making the first approach was maintained in a Chat

Room environment. However, it was not clear how many females were actually in the Chat Rooms. The females certainly received a lot of attention in Chat Rooms, perhaps that is because they are perceived as rare. Unlike real-world interactions, initial cyber greetings were likely to be sexual, sometimes hostile, and usually aggressive. If the length of the trials were extended, females would be likely to be propositioned more. Challenges to extending the trial length would be maintaining a consistent script.

Study 2: Sexy vs. Non-Sexy Screen Names

Study 2 expands on Study 1's paradigm, differing in the types of screen names utilized. This study investigated if the perceived "Sexiness" of the Screen Names would affect the Time Until Response or the aggressiveness of the responses.

Methods

Materials

Chat Rooms: For uniformity between Studies, the same Chat Rooms used in Study 1 were utilized in this expansion (http://www.chat-avenue.com).

Screen Names: "Sexy" screen names were chosen from the most popular adult movie actors and actresses of 2008-2009, the rationale being that adult performers choose their stage names to come across as sexy to their audience. "Non-Sexy" screen names were chosen from the most popular baby names from the 1900's that were no longer listed in current popular baby names. These names are no longer in use and people were expected to associate them with older aged adults who may not meet our current cultural definition of sexy (Table 3).

Table 3: Sample "Sexy/Non Sexy" Male and "Sexy/Non Sexy" Female Screen Names Used

Sexy Female Screen Names	Non-sexy Female Screen Names	Sexy Male Screen Names	Non-sexy Male Screen Names
Alexis	Myrtle	Randy	Lester
Brianna	Ethel	Lex	Sherman
Jayden	Mildred	Rocky	Melvin
Brandi	Eleanor	Evan	Philbert
Amy	Gladys	Jack	Clarence
Raven	Bertha	Kurt	Virgil
Bree	Agnes	Allen	Luther

Procedure

Confederates entered the Chat Rooms using different types of screen names ("Sexy" Female vs. "Non-Sexy" Female and "Sexy" Male vs. "Non-Sexy" Male). As in Study 1, the confederates in Study 2 engaged in conversation with the first respondent to private message producing 1 respondent per trial. There were 12 trials with the "Non Sexy" Male Screen Names, 21 trials with the "Non Sexy" Female Screen Names, 21 trials with the "Sexy" Male Screen names, and 18 trials with the "Sexy" Female Screen names. In one minute intervals, confederates conversed with the chat room holding to a script to convey presence (see Figure 1 listed in Study 1). The same procedures were used from Study 1.

Results

A MANOVA with IVs of Sex and "Sexy" vs. "Non-Sexy" Screen Names and DVs of Time Until First Response and Proposition was run. There was a Multivariate main effect for Sex, $F(1,68) = 211.32$, $p < 0.001$. Female screen names were contacted significantly more quickly than Male Screen Names for private messages. There were no Multivariate main effect for "Sexiness" but there was a significant multivariate interaction, $F(2,36) = 6.12$, $p < 0.05$. There was a possible interaction trend $F(1,68) = 3.24$, $p = .076$. Examination of the interaction revealed that "Non-Sexy" Female Screen Names were contacted quicker than the "Sexy" Female Screen Names, while the opposite trend appeared for the Male Screen Names (as seen in Figure 2 below).

Figure 2: Time Until First Response

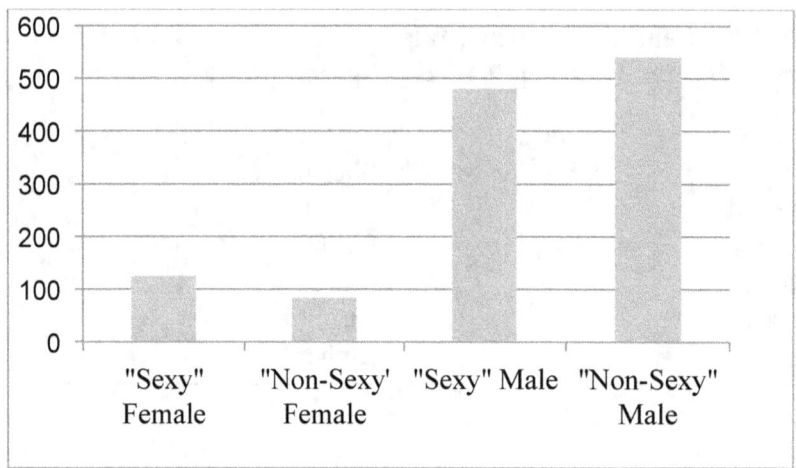

There was also a significant ANOVA with sex as the IV and Proposition as the DV, $F(1,70) = 47.57$, $p < 0.001$. Females were significantly more likely to be propositioned for sex than males (Figure 3).

Figure 3 Percentage of Proposition

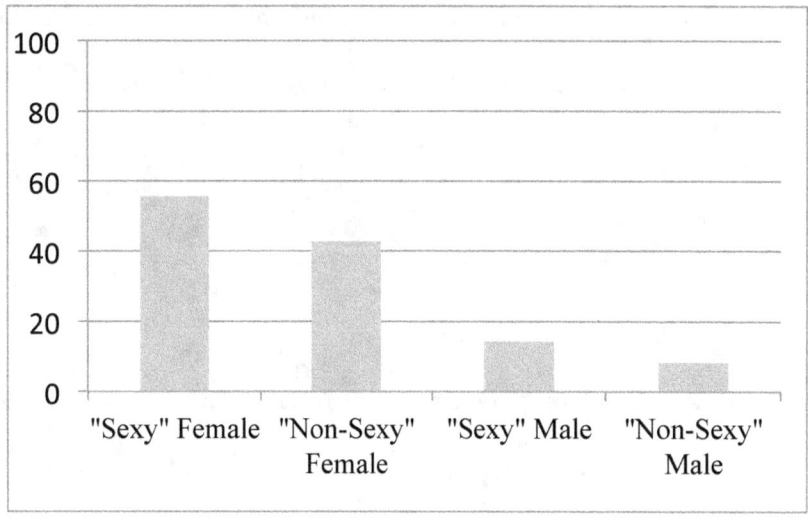

Discussion

Females were contacted more quickly than males which replicated Study 1's findings (Serafino et al., 2010). We did not find support for the idea that "Sexy" names would elicit quicker interactions than "Non-Sexy" names. Possibly the "Sexy" names were not sexy enough or the "Non-Sexy" names needed to be less sexy. We believe the interaction trend that approached significance may show that the sexiness of the Screen Name was important for male Screen Names but not for Female Screen Names. "Sexy" male names were contacted quicker than "Non-Sexy" male names. Males received much less attention and the sexiness of the name may have given them an advantage. For females, "Non-Sexy" names were contacted more quickly, possibly because respondents hoped these females would be more receptive or because the "Non-Sexy" names are more noticeable. Future studies need to include additional trials to verify if there is an actual interaction. If the interaction holds true, the cause of the interaction would be the next question to examine.

Females were more likely to be propositioned than males and the Male Screen Names that were propositioned were always propositioned by other males. Common requests were for a variety of types of cyber sex, as well as requests for video chat or pictures. Respondents were substantially more aggressive and used language that could have resulted in a sexual harassment lawsuit if used in the real world.

Study 3: Hobby vs. Paraphilic Screen Names

While running the previous 2 studies we noted there were very explicit Screen Names that tended to refer to sexual preferences as well as more innocent Screen Names referring to people's hobbies. We wondered if these explicit Screen Names that we documented were treated differently than the hobby Screen Names on these websites. This Study also tracked total number of responses to each screen name as well as response times of first confederate.

Methods

Respondents

There were 741 responses counted for the entire study. Only 2 responses were for the Male Screen Names, the remaining 739 responded to the Female Screen Names.

Materials

Chat Rooms: For uniformity between Studies, the same Chat Rooms used in Studies 1 and 2 were utilized in this expansion (http://www.chat-avenue.com).

Screen Names: Four types of screen names were used: Male and Female Hobby Screen Names and Male and Female

Paraphilic Screen Names. The Hobby Screen Names simply contained a word or phrase related to various hobbies and activities. The Paraphilic Screen Names were created to represent various paraphilias and utilized puns and double entendres to express the desired paraphilia. These were modeled on the screen names that we had observed being used on the Chat Rooms. None of the names were particularly extreme or out of the norm for what was being used in the Chat Rooms. Every Screen Name was prefaced my "Mr." or "Miss" to indicate sex (Table 4).

Table 4: Sample Hobby and Paraphilic Screen Names

Male Hobby Screen Names	Female Hobby Screen Names	Male Paraphilic Screen Names	Female Paraphilic Screen Names
Mr. Artist	Miss Artist	Mr. Necromance	Miss Necromance
Mr. Comedy	Miss Comedy	Mr. Furvert	Miss Furvert
Mr. Swimmer	Miss Swimmer	Mr. GrannyGroper	Miss GrampaGroper
Mr. ReadsAlot	Miss ReadsAlot	Mr. Ballsagna	Miss Ballsagna
Mr. Videogamer	Miss Videogamer	Mr. Pain	Miss Pain

Procedures

The same basic procedure from Studies 1 and 2 was adhered to including the script (see Figure 1). The main difference was tracking the number of Private Message Requests without interacting with any of the respondents. This decision was made because we noted in the previous studies that some Screen Names received and continued to receive additional requests for private messages. Study 3 uses Number of Private Message Requests as a measure of popularity.

Results

An ANOVA was run with sex (males and females) as the independent variable and Proposition as the dependent variable, $F(1,70) = 47.57$, $p < 0.001$. Female Screen Names received more private message requests than Male Screen Names, regardless of whether they were provocative or hobby-related. A MANOVA was run using Hobby vs. Paraphilic Screen Name and Chat Room as the IVs and the Number of Private Message Requests as the DV. Females (19.22) received significantly more responses than males (.06), $F(1,71) = 115.62$, $p < 0.001$. A MANOVA was run using Hobby vs. Paraphilic Screen Name and Chat Room as the IVs and Time of First Response as the DV. Females (73.22 sec.) received significantly quicker first response times than males (296 sec.), $F(1,71) = 618.5$, $p < 0.001$. There were no significant differences found between types of names, even though they were very different in their nature. Once again, the main finding is that females receive more attention. Both Paraphilic Screen Names and Hobby-

Related Screen Names made the top 10 list for most popular and quickest response (see Figure 4).

Figure 4

Most Popular Screen Names	Time of First Response (sec.)
Mistress of Pain	9
Miss Videogamer	10
Miss Squirts […]	10
Miss Runner	18
Miss Photographer	18
Miss Swimmer	25
Miss Classical	29
Miss Oops […]	30
Miss Ballsagna	33
Miss Necromance	33

Most Popular Screen Names	Number of Responses
Miss Cougar	46
Miss PampersPlaything	42
Miss Jazz	35
Miss Country	35
Miss Cushion4Pushin	33
Miss Swimmer	31
Miss Sport	30
Miss Videogamer	29
Miss Hiker	27
Miss Runner	27

Discussion

Study 3 replicated the findings of both Study 1 and Study 2. Females received more Private Message Requests than Males, regardless of whether their Screen Name was provocative or Hobby-Related. As they say, one occurrence is a phenomenon, two is a coincidence, but three is a pattern. Additional trials were run chatting with first respondents but no significance was found.

Conclusions

Having run these studies across 3 years' time and encountering the same Screen Names in all 3 studies, these Chat Rooms appear to be a community with relatively stable membership. Unfortunately, we have very little idea of who the actual people behind the Screen Names are. It is unclear whether the interactions we observed are replacing these individuals' real-world social interactions or if they are a sign of dissatisfaction with their real-world relationships. Or is there a beneficial aspect? Are these virtual worlds important for creating social outlets and utilizing fantasy to help them grow in their creativity? There is not a reliable way of getting actual information from the members of these online communities without violating their privacy and violating the terms and conditions of the websites. There may be ways of getting more information about the community as a whole. Online, we found that the majority of respondents reported being tall, athletic, Australian males with interesting colored eyes and generous endowments of all kinds. We could test the demographic percentages against the actual distributions in the real world. For example, we could gather data and find out how tall people in the Chat Room claim to be and compare that average to the real-world norms. We are also suspicious about the large quantity of Australians who appear to be in the Chat Rooms at time periods that are unlikely for actual Australians to be active. One way of testing the validity of their proposed location would be to ask them questions about small surrounding towns. Another way would be to ask them what vehicle they drive. A lot of people may not realize that many cars that are readily available in America are not available abroad. Though they are capable of import, the average person is not going to have the means to import a vehicle from abroad.

There appeared to be fewer females in these Chat Rooms and a high desire from males to interact with them. It would be interesting to see how many of the females in Chat Rooms are actually females. We could investigate this by asking questions about female lifestyles that males would generally be unaware of (e.g. popular mascara brands, Barbie's best friend, etc).

Although this would probably be too dangerous to run, it would be interesting to see if the propositions used online would be tolerated in a real-world setting. Not to mention, none of the male confederates are willing to put themselves on the line for this paradigm.

Another anomaly is that many respondents report being college males but few college students of the experimenters' acquaintanceship admitted to being familiar or using the Chat Rooms. Do college students frequent these Chat Rooms but not admit it to their friends or are the online individuals lying about their age?

The aggressive and sexual nature of these Chat Rooms may explain the lack of females involved. It is very easy to avoid any type of cyber harassment or bullying by simply not logging on to the websites. The question then becomes, what draws the people who frequent the websites to spend so much time? The anonymity allows people to express themselves in a perceived safe environment without filters and without worries of appearing "extreme".

References

Haby, J., Serafino, A. B. & Sia, T. L. (2011). *Wanna Cyber Again? Does a Rose named Myrtle smell as sweet?* Poster presentation at the 57th Anual Southwest Psychological Association Confrence, San Anotnio, Texas.

Kraut, R., Patterson, M., Lundmark, V., Kiesler, S., Mukophadhyay, T., & Scherlis, W. (1998). Internet paradox: A social technology that reduces social involvement and psychological well-being? *American Psychologist*, 53(9), 1017-1031.

Rollman, J. B., Krug, K., & Parente, F. (2000). The chat room phenomenon: Reciprocal communication in cyberspace. *Cyber Psychology & Behavior*, 3(2), 161-166.

Serafino, A. B., Haby, J., Sia, T. L., & Czuchry, M. L. (2010). *Wanna Cyber? The effect of percieved gender on interactions within chat rooms.* Poster presentation at the 56th Anual Southwest Psychological Association Confrence, Dallas, Texas.

3 There are some things you just don't share: Adventures on ChatRoulette

By

Nathan J. Fry, Catherine R. Hoffmann, Kyle A. Leihsing, Canaan A. Hoffmann, & Tiffiny L. Sia, Ph.D.

Special Acknowledgements: Andrew Serafino for creating the paradigm, Andrew Serafino and Morgan Hale for being confederates through grueling trials, Jeremy Pfenninger for being extremely meticulous with data collection, and Morgan Hale for work in data analysis.

Abstract

Previous research has suggested that pathological Internet communities do exist but previous research has not found the methodology (Durkin et al., 2006). Previous research has been done to find these communities by logging into chat rooms which resulted in female usernames and users being subjected to explicit and demanding attention as compared to male names and users (Serafino et.al., 2010). Video Chat Rooms offer a visual as well as a verbal component that create a more personal interaction, while still remaining anonymous. However late night comedy shows have been making jokes about the usage of video chat for more deviant behavior such as exhibitionism. Two studies were run to try to identify what and why people use video chat rooms. Study one thought talking to the people on the chat rooms such as ChatRoulette (targeted for the heterosexual population) or PinkRoulette (targeted for the homosexual population) might be an innovative methodology for documenting video chats and to see if the media hype was accurate. The variable of Traditional (normal dress) vs. Counterculture (non-traditional dress) was added as well to see how appearance manipulated the amount of interactions the researchers were exposed to. Based on that study on both ChatRoulette and PinkRoulette it showed that the female confederates, if they do not terminate the conversation, are subjected to more explicit attention when compared to males on the same site (Serafino et.al, 2011). The appearance of the confederate also showed significant difference in how much time the confederate was talked to. The female when dressed in Counterculture attire had more interaction time and the male had more interaction time when dressed in Traditional attire. This led into a second study in which two confederates terminated the conversation whenever the material became too explicit or were subjugated to sexual proposals so that they could look for the availability of normal social interactions without being exposed for prolonged instances of explicit material. For both studies ANOVAs were conducted using three independent variables and one dependent variable. In study one the independent variables were Culture (Traditional vs. Counter-Culture), Sex (Male vs. Female), and Chat Room (Chat Roulette vs. Pink Roulette), and interaction time was the dependent variable. For study two the independent variables were Culture (Dressed Up vs. Dressed Down), Sex (Male vs. Female), and Chat Room (Chat Roulette vs. Pink Roulette), and interaction time was the dependent variable. This analysis showed that female confederates also received longer interaction replicating the findings of study one. There was also a difference in amount of time the people talked with the confederates depending on which site the confederate was on, with Chat Roulette interaction time being longer. Unlike the first study though the appearance of the confederate did not make a difference in the amount of time the confederate was talked to.

Key Words: *Chat, Chat Rooms, Online Communities, Exhibitionism*

There are some things you just don't share: Adventures on ChatRoulette

Social interaction is drastically changing in the world. People are beginning to spend as much, if not more, time interacting with people over the Internet. Online communities that emulate and attempt to imitate face to face interactions have been growing, and it is important to understand how people use these communities to engage socially, as well as the methods that are used to do so. Previous research has suggested that pathological Internet communities do exist (Durkin et al., 2006). Durkin's study supported the idea that there is evidence towards a higher use of social media, although there has not been a lot of research on the subject matter. However, this does stress the idea that social interaction may be changing and the methodology of these interactions should be explored. While the Durkin study did not find the methodology for online communities, preliminary research was conducted on verbal chat rooms that suggests that female usernames are subjected to explicit and demanding attention as compared to male names (Serafino et.al, 2010; Serafino et.al, 2011). This type of information is key in understanding the direction that social media will take human interaction. The frequency of which females (or perceived to be females) will receive negative types of attention suggests that males in society are more open in online communities than they might be in face-to-face interactions. It may also lead to fewer females engaging in online communities which could cause a potential social gap between sexes to happen.

Video Chat Rooms offer a visual as well as a verbal component that create a more personal interaction, while still remaining anonymous. The current studies built upon the methodology of preliminary research but used a video chat room (Serafino et.al, 2011). However late night comedy shows have been making jokes about the usage of video chat for more deviant behavior such as exhibitionism. The paper explores two independently run studies; one that examined if the chat rooms would be an innovative methodology for documenting video chats and to see if the media hype was accurate, and a second study in which confederates terminated the conversation whenever the material became explicit or were subjugated to sexual proposals, so that they could look for the availability of normal social interactions without being exposed to prolonged explicit material.

Study one examines what types of interactions people might encounter on both the ChatRoulette and PinkRoulette websites. Because they are targeted towards different audiences, an initial thought would be that certain people would be favored on the two websites over others. This can be tracked by how quickly someone in the chat room would "instant-next" (immediately hit the next button, thus ending the interaction) another person. ChatRoulette, being targeted towards a heterosexual audience, would have males on it who are more receptive towards females, while PinkRoulette, being targeted towards a homosexual audience, would have males be more receptive towards males.

Study two explores how often a more "normal" interaction may occur on the Chat and PinkRoulette websites. Although subjects would still "instant-next" the confederates, confederates would also terminate any conversations that were offensive. Confederates would engage in conversation with any partners that wished to talk. Between the times of study one and study two, additional security measures were added in order to reduce the amount of exhibitionist behavior that appeared on the ChatRoulette website, although PinkRoulette has not followed suit.

Study 1

Method

Participants

Participants were used in the online chat rooms from various parts of the world. The two websites that were chosen were ChatRoulette and PinkRoulette. Every participant was randomly selected through the website itself and by agreeing to the terms of the website they consequently consented to interactions. In total, there were 244 participants with 177 (72.5%) males, 17 (6.9%) females, and 50 (20%) unknown. The unknown participants were those that did not have their camera on or were out of view from their camera but initiated conversation with the confederates.

Materials

Three confederates were used: A male dressed traditionally, a male dressed non-traditionally (counter-culture), and a male dressed as a traditional female and a non-traditional (counter-culture) female.

Male   **Male**   **Female**   **Female**

Traditional   **Counter-Culture**   **Traditional**   **Counter-Culture**

*One of the experimenters dressed as a Female facsimile in order to avoid having to recruit a female confederate for a role that might involve explicit material and potential sexual harassment. Special care was taken to make sure that the confederate looked the part as a real female.

Observers would use a checklist that tracked various aspects of the trial, including the participant number, sex of the participant, whether the participant was visible, race of the participant, and the time taken to complete the trial.

Figure 1: Observer Checklist

General Observations and timekeeping sheet

    Target #___   Instant Next Off-cam   M F   group Time (secs)___

    Target #___   Instant Next Off-cam   M F   group Time (secs)___

    Target #___   Instant Next Off-cam   M F   group Time (secs)___

Specific Observer Checklist

    Target #___   M   F   Alone   Pair   Group

    White   Black   Hispanic   Other_____

    Teen   Adult   Middle Age   Other

    0=normal dress 1=proactive/unconventional   2=shirtless 3=nude 4=exhibitionism

    0_____1_____2_____3_____4_____5_____6_____7_____8_____9_____10

    not attractive   Attractive

    0_____1_____2_____3_____4_____5_____6_____7_____8_____9_____10

    Not Flirtatious   Flirtatious

    0_____1_____2_____3_____4_____5_____6_____7_____8_____9_____10

    Aggressive   Friendly

    Comments: (Comments included descriptions of behaviors as well as content of chat)

Procedures

A confederate would log onto one of the websites (Chat or PinkRoulette) and keep a neutral non-judgmental face and chat via keyboard with whoever was randomly assigned through the website. A second monitor was connected to the confederate's computer to allow the observers to view trials unseen by the participant. There was one general observer and two specific observers. After every 10 trials observers would compare to make sure they were coding consistently. Although we could hear participants, we disabled our microphone to avoid cross-talk from observers being heard. The interactions would last as long as the participants wished them to, unless the participants mentioned or appeared to be underage, in which case we would "instant next." The interactions initially had no time limit, but for practical reasons a maximum time of ten minutes was then created so that conversation could ensue for a reasonable period of time. This allowed trials to run faster and more efficiently.

Results

An ANOVA was conducted with 3 Independent variables: Culture (Traditional vs. Counter-Culture), Sex (Male vs. Female), and Chat Room (Chat Roulette vs. Pink Roulette) and interaction time as the dependent variable. There was a main effect for sex with females (M=173.02 seconds) having longer interactions than males (M=50.76 seconds), $F(1,269)=29.10$, $p<0.0001$.

Figure 2: Main Effect for Confederate Sex

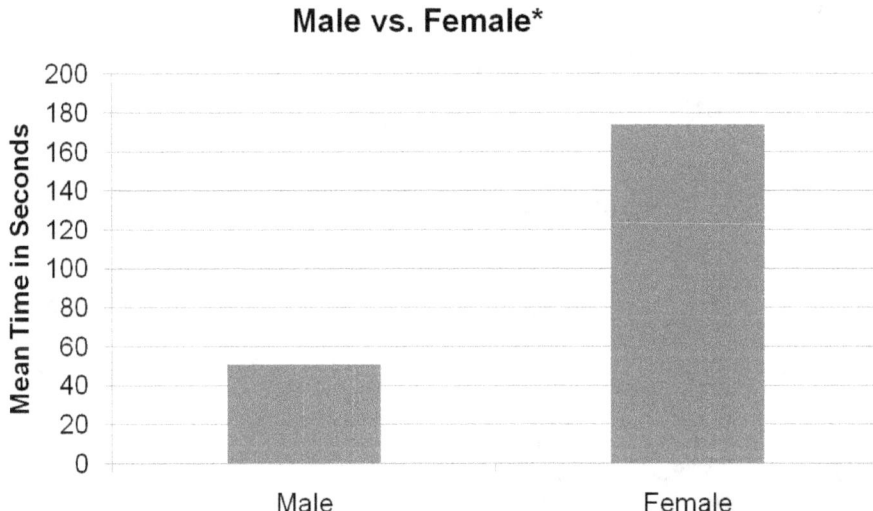

Counter-Culture(CC) Females received longer interaction times than Traditional Females, while traditional Males received longer interaction times than Counter-Culture males, $F(1,269)=5.04$, $p<0.05$.

Figure 3: Interaction between Culture & Confederate Sex

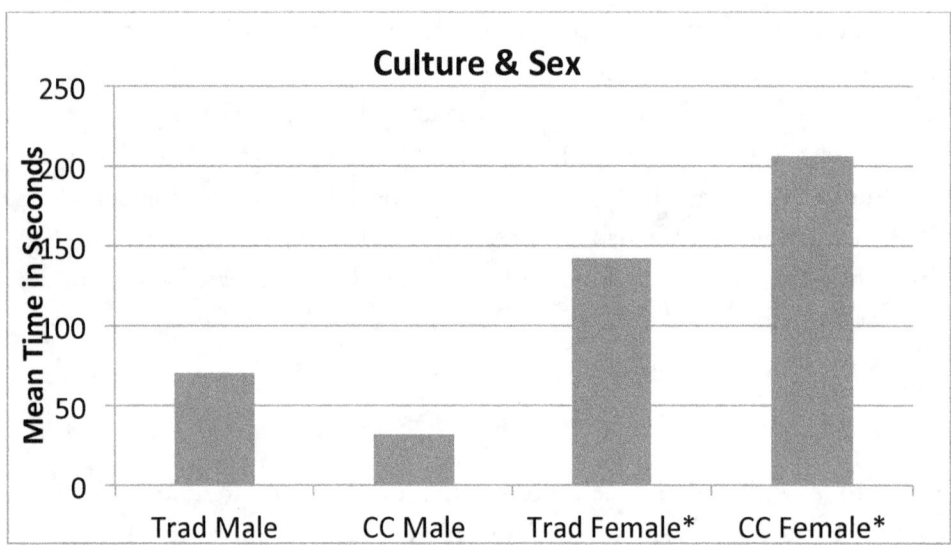

Traditional Confederates received longer interaction times than Counter-Culture confederates in pink roulette, but counter culture received longer interaction times than traditional confederates in Chat Roulette, $F(1,269)=4.44$, $p<0.05$.

Figure 4: Interaction between Culture & Chat Room

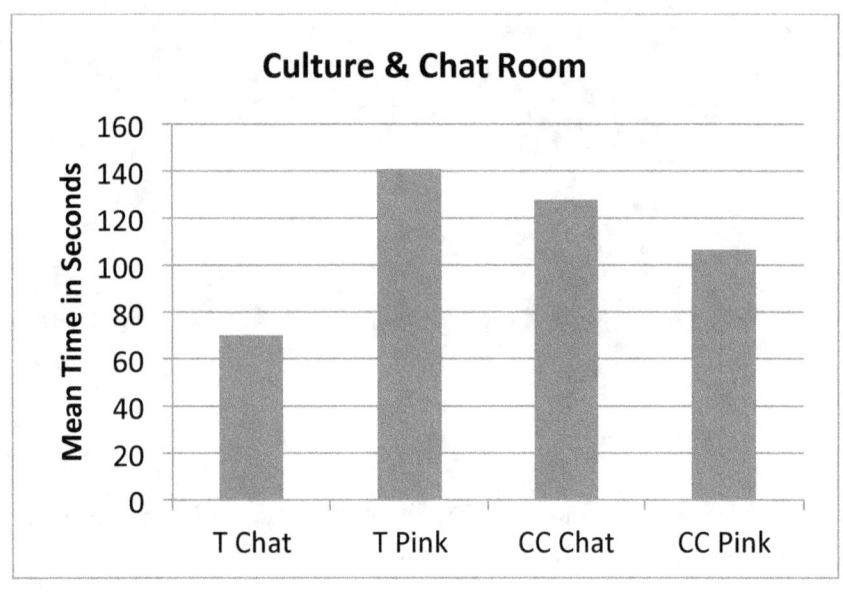

Discussion

Males vs. Females

The female confederate received significantly longer interaction times, probably because of the scarcity of females on the sites (90% males).

When the female confederate would start a conversation the participant seemed relieved and excited to see a female on the screen. It could be all the hype of exhibitionism has frightened all the females away from these types of randomly assigned video chat rooms. So when the female was on the screen the participant would take up more time talking to her due to the rarity of females on the site.

Culture vs. Sex

The confederates who are the most different from the usual clientele for each particular chat room received the longest interactions.

The difference of the attire seemed to make people overall want to talk to the confederate longer unless the confederate was a male. The female confederate reported being sexually harassed (usually requests to remove items of clothing) more when in the counterculture attire which leads the researchers to believe that a stereotype exists of the non-traditional looking females are believed to be more sexually promiscuous. The participants seemed to believe that if they repeated their demands more frequently that they would be successful.

The male confederate did receive less interaction time when dressed in counterculture attire. It could be that he seemed intimidating and could have frightened people which led to a shorter interaction time.

Culture vs. Chat Rooms

There was a difference in how much interaction time the confederate received on the two sites based upon the type of attire the participant was wearing.

On the ChatRoulette site the confederates had a significantly longer interaction time if they were dressed in Counter-Culture attire. This could be a result of the site having such a large audience that novelty of the Counter-Culture is appealing. The familiarity of the normal day to day person may be boring to the participant which allows conversation with the Counter-Culture confederates to result in a longer interaction time.

On the PinkRoulette site the Traditional dressed confederates received longer interaction time than the Counter-Culture attire confederates. The earlier section discussed the stereotype of the Counter-Culture female as perceived as more promiscuous. On this site there were more instances of exhibitionism which leads the researchers to believe this site may be more promiscuous. The assumptions of the participants that the Counter-Culture confederate is more promiscuous makes the Traditional confederate the novel person to interact with. This would lead to more interest and longer interaction times.

If this is the case that would strengthen the stereotype that the Counter-Culture attire would lead people to believe that this attire means that a person is more sexually permissible than a person dressed in traditional attire.

Conclusions

There was a difference in how long participants talked to the confederates based upon sex, attire, and which video chat room was being used. Overall the female participant was talked to more but when broken down, certain factors resulted in different interaction times.

More research can be done to find more of these variables that change the interaction times and see to track the websites users to see if their voyeuristic behavior decreases or becomes extinct over a period of time.

If the study was to be done again a real female confederate could be used if a way was made to cut down more of the explicit variables that made these websites controversial and popular.

Challenges

Because we continued the conversations with anyone who wanted to talk to us, we may have ended up with the more extreme participants who were used to being "instant-nexted". It is possible that their objective was to shock or offend the confederates, but since our confederates were keeping a neutral face, this objective would not be met. Likewise, because we remained with the first participant that wanted to talk with us, there may have been more "normal" conversations that could have happened, thus creating a participant bias in our methodology. We wanted to examine the degree to which a normal interaction may occur on the two video chat websites. Because we were going to "instant-next" all offensive material that may occur, a female confederate that was warned about the possibility of such interactions happening was able to be a part of the next study.

Study 2

Method

Participants

Participants were used from online chat rooms in various parts of the world. The two chat rooms were ChatRoulette and PinkRoulette. Every participant was randomly selected through the website itself and by agreeing to the terms of the website they consequently consented to their identity being used for this study. In total there were 292 participants with 251 (85.96%) males, 16 (5.48%) females, and 25 unknown (8.56%) that remained out of view but initiated conversation.

Materials

Two confederates were used: A male dressed up or dressed down, and a female dressed up or dressed down.

Male Dressed Up   **Male Dressed Down**   **Female Dressed Up**   **Female Dressed Down**

Observers would use a checklist that tracked various aspects of the trial, including the participant number, sex of the participant, whether the participant was visible, raced of the participant, and the time taken to complete the trial.

Figure 5: Observer Checklist

General Observations and timekeeping sheet

Target #___   Instant Next   Off-cam   M   F   group   Time (secs)___

Target #___   Instant Next   Off-cam   M   F   group   Time (secs)___

Target #___   Instant Next   Off-cam   M   F   group   Time (secs)___

Specific Observer Checklist

Target #___   M   F   Alone   Pair   Group

White   Black   Hispanic   Other_____

Teen   Adult   Middle Age   Other

0=normal dress   1=proactive/unconventional   2=shirtless   3=nude   4=exhibitionism

0____1____2____3____4____5____6____7____8____9____10

not attractive   Attractive

0____1____2____3____4____5____6____7____8____9____10

Not Flirtatious   Flirtatious

0____1____2____3____4____5____6____7____8____9____10

Aggressive   Friendly

Comments: (Comments included descriptions of behaviors as well as content of chat)

Procedures

The confederate would log onto one of the two video chat rooms that randomly assign partners and span the globe were used: ChatRoulette which serves a general audience and PinkRoulette which serves a homosexual audience. Confederates logged onto one of the websites and kept a non-judgmental face while chatting with whoever was randomly assigned. Observers viewed the interactions while remaining out of view of the web camera. One observer tracked length of interaction and a second observer tracked the demographics of the partners. Trials lasted until the partner "instant-nexted", displayed explicit language/behavior, or 10 minutes of chat was reached. Criteria for a confederate hitting "instant-next" were if the partner was underage, presented graphic exhibitions, or if the confederate was propositioned in a sexual manner. One of the main differences between study one and study two is the ability to skip someone if those criterion are met. This allowed this study to have a real female confederate instead of a male dressed as a female.

Results

An ANOVA was conducted with 3 independent variables: Culture (Dressed Up vs. Dressed Down), Sex (Male vs. Female), and Chat Room (Chat Roulette vs. Pink Roulette) and interaction time as the dependent variable.

There was a main effect for sex with the females (M=135.79 seconds) having longer interaction than males (M=26.03); $F_{(1, 277)}=31.08$, $p<0.0001$.

Figure 6: Main effect for Interaction time of Confederate Sex

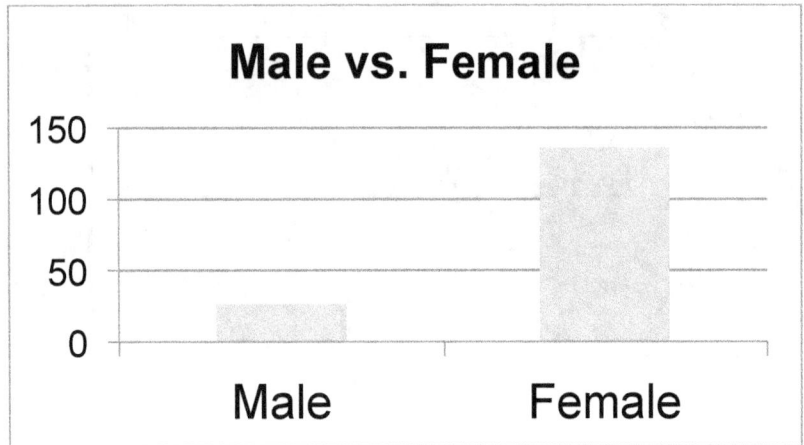

There was a main effect for the amount of time the trials lasted with Chat Roulette (M=114.44 seconds) and Pink Roulette (M=48.01), $F_{(1,277)}= 11.167$, $p<0.05$.

Figure 7: Main Effect for Trial Time & Chat Room

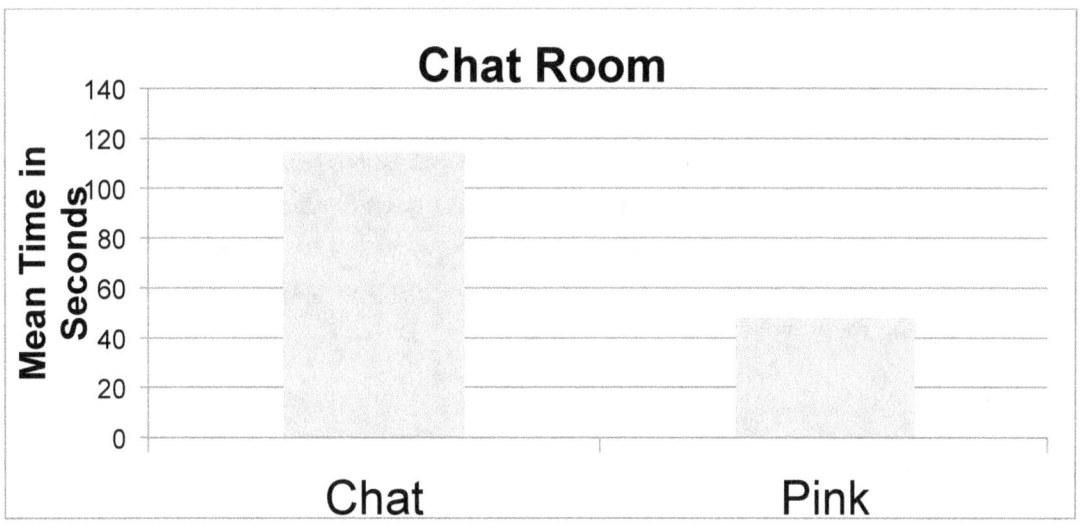

The Female Confederate received longer interaction times than male confederates F (1,277)=16.756, $p<0.0001$.

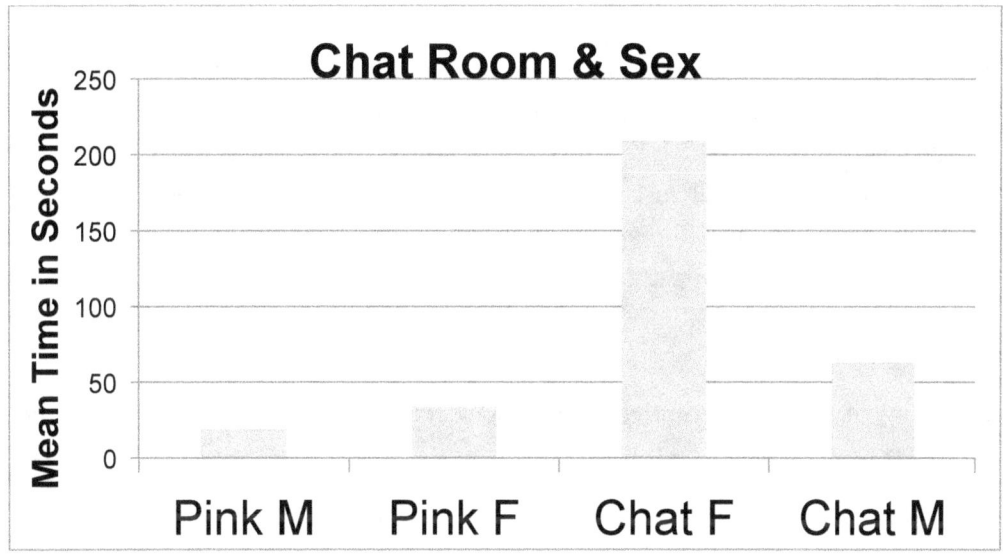

A MANOVA was conducted with the sex of confederate (male vs. female) and Chat Room (ChatRoulette vs. PinkRoulette) as the independent variables and the likelihood of the confederate "instant-nexting" the partner and the likelihood of the partner "instant-nexting" the confederate as the dependent variables. There was a main effect for sex showing that males were "instant-nexted" significantly more than females in both chat rooms, F(1,275) = 23.48, $p<0.0001$.

Discussion

Male vs. Female

The female confederate also received longer interactions, replicating the findings of study one.

This strengthens the earlier finding about how the online video chat rooms have fewer females on them than males. Like in the first study when presented with a female the confederate when make seemed excited and wanting to have some kind of interaction with a female. Also the theory that males engaged in longer conversations with the female confederate as so to "warm them up" before propositioning them to increase their chance of the female showing them what they ask for.

ChatRoulette vs. PinkRoulette

There was a difference in amount of time the people talked with the confederates depending on which site the confederate was on. Chat Roulette had a longer interaction time than Pink Roulette. This might be because Chat Roulette is known to be more of a social site and a more popular site.

Chat Room & Sex

The difference that happened here was that the female confederate was talked to significantly longer than the male confederate in the ChatRoulette chat room and in the PinkRoulette chat room.

This could be that the people on Chat Roulette are looking for females and will talk to one for a longer time. With the PinkRoulette site, the surprising find that the female was talked to longer when it is targeted for the homosexual community and many of the users on this site were male that chatted with the female. One reason for this could be that the people who usually use ChatRoulette may have become bored and are using other sites to find females to converse with. Perhaps the males were willing to have conversations with her because they were not considering her for propositions.

Dressed Up vs. Dressed Down

There was no difference in amount of interaction time the confederate received when split by the attire they were wearing.

Unlike the other study where there was an interaction in attire, this showed no difference. This may be because of the types of dress chosen and it not being as different as the Traditional vs. Counter-Culture. Also both dress types are familiar to the participants so comfort levels should not be that different when comparing the two against each other. The stereotype that the counterculture held of being promiscuous was gone and it resulted in no difference in how long people interacted with the confederates based upon dress.

Conclusions

The same conclusion that females have significantly more interaction time found in the Serafino study was replicated (Serafino et.al, 2011). People on ChatRoulette chatted longer than people on PinkRoulette. When it came to both chat rooms, the male confederate was "nexted" more than the female confederate, it appeared that the partners were looking for females to chat with. However females were forced to next many partners due to explicit material in order to find conversations. In addition, several conversations were aimed at warming up the confederate for proposition. Making friends does not seem to be the predominate goal for websites like PinkRoulette and ChatRoulette. Perhaps this is due to the anonymous nature of the websites. If there were websites that were local and got rid of the anonymity of these websites maybe the behavior would clean up and the more friends would develop.

Challenges

ChatRoulette is creating software to limit exhibitionistic behavior midway through trials in the second study. They implemented different security, although Pink Roulette has not followed suit.

Future Studies

One area of further research could interview the exhibitionists on ChatRoulette. Although we didn't formally do this, several people comment that they do this online several times a day. One individual commented that he also would like to be nude in public. However, this person was from a country where nude beaches and parks are more common.

Cross-cultural observations could also be made possible by choosing time zones to target. This would allow an examination of the variance between cultures online interactions. One challenge to this paradigm is language difficulty. We did have several trials in which we were unable to communicate due to a lack of common language. These trials are more likely to occur in early hours of the morning (2 or 3 a.m.). It took us a while to realize that at certain times we were encountering more Asian or Middle Eastern participants because it was a more normal time of day for them.

Another future study could look at different ages of participants on the video chat websites and how differently they interact from one another. It was fairly common to see middle-aged men. We seldom encountered middle-aged or older females. It would be interesting to see if middle-aged females were treated differently than younger females, particularly, if the middle-aged females received more respect.

A future study could also examine the differences of interactions based on race, which was a factor that was looked at in a Criaglist study (Garcia et.al, 2011). It would be beneficial to recruit African American and Hispanic confederates to run trials. Another layer could be having our confederates dress stereotypically for their race. In-group participants might exhibit more hostility towards the stereotypically dressed confederates because they are reinforcing a negative stereotype of the race the respondents share. It would also be interesting to find out if people are more likely to exhibit prejudicial behavior online than in person.

Another study could examine differences in interactions based on sexual orientation of confederates (gay males or lesbian females). In this case, it might be easier to have couples on screen holding hands, although we could have participants dress stereotypically. A confound is that some cultures we might encounter view men and or women holding hands as an appropriate social gesture and we would not want our confederates to have to engage in more extreme behavior. It is also not clear how a heterosexual couple on Chat and PinkRoulette would be received. Would they be viewed as more likely to be seeking normal conversation, or would they receive more propositions than an individual or a homosexual couple?

Regardless, it is clear that sites like Chat and PinkRoulette have much different social norms than non-online communities. The degree to which interactions on these sites are beneficial or harmful to the user is not yet clear, and should be examined with further research. We found disturbing behaviors as well as "caring" conversations between the confederates and participants.

References

Durkin, Keith., Forsyth, Craig J., Quinn, James F.(2006). *Pathological Internet Communities: a new direction for sexual deviance research in a post modern era.* Sociological Spectrum 26 (6) 595-606

Serafino, A. B., Haby, J., Sia, T. L., & Czuchry, M. L. (2010). *Wanna cyber? The effect of perceived gender on interactions within chat rooms.* Poster presented at the 56th Annual Southwestern Psychological Association Conference, Dallas, Texas.

Serafino, A.B., Hale, M., Sia T.L., Pfenninger J. & Hoffmann, C. A., (2011) *Chat Roulette: Effects of Sex and Appearance on Interactions in Video Chat-rooms.* Poster accepted to be presented at 57th Annual Southwestern Psychological Association Conference, San Antonio, Texas.

Haby J., Serafino, A.B. & Sia T.L. (2011). *Wanna Cyber Again? Does a Rose named Myrtle smell as sweet?* Poster accepted to be presented at 57th Annual Southwestern Psychological Association Conference, San Antonio, Texas.

Garcia, Z.M., Leihsing K., Schmoekel, T., Rincon J.A., Hoffmann, C. & Sia, T.L. (2011*). Craigslist Poetry Slam: Reactions to Breaking Stereotypes of Sex and Race.* Poster submitted to be presented at 57th Annual Southwestern Psychological Association Conference, Oklahoma City, OK.

4 Social Media Conversations About
Sexist Breast Cancer Awareness Campaigns

By

Elizabeth Beck-Dietert

Research Question

I started my research project with an interest in whether the "I like it" campaigns found on

Facebook which were circulated by women in an attempt to raise awareness for breast cancer have been

successful in increasing breast cancer research, funding or education. However as I proceeded in my search

a new question emerged, "What is the effect of campaigns like "I like it". The "I like it" campaigns have

gone viral on Facebook through the use of sexually charged speech. These campaigns have harnessed

sexually charged speech to in an attempt to raise awareness for breast cancer, despite the fact that they are

not associated with the National Breast Cancer Awareness Month and that they have little to nothing to do

with breast cancer research, fund raising, or education. Campaigns which sexualize cancer like "I like it",

"Don't let cancer steal second base!", "Save the Ta-Tas!" and others have raised the ire of some who feel

the campaigns "exclude the women they are designed to support" and encourage female "buy in" to being

objectified in the name of supporting breast cancer research. Social media is facilitating a debate over

whether "I like it" and other sexualized breast cancer awareness campaigns are helping in the fight against

breast cancer by encouraging and supporting women (and men) who are battling for their lives or whether these campaigns simply what Evgeny Morozov would call "slactivisim" (activity which gives the one engaged the feeling of doing something without actually doing anything) which does little more than reinforce entrenched hegemonic ideas that objectify women and trivialize women's health.

Research Plan

In this research project I studied articles about the Facebook viral breast cancer awareness campaigns as well as the comment threads associated with these articles, Facebook threads involved in these posts and blogs as well as the conversations associated with the blogs to document the debate over sexualized breast cancer awareness campaigns facilitated by social media. The data documented that a debate exists over the effect of these campaigns have on breast cancer awareness and respect for women in general. I also looked at Judith Butler's theory of the politics of the performative and discussed the application of reclamation of language and the work that Antonio Gramsci's did in the theory of hegemony to frame the issues on both sides of the debate. Finally I looked at some of the arguments surrounding the sexualized breast cancer awareness campaigns which fit Evgeny Morozov's idea of "slactivisim" with regard to effectiveness or ineffectiveness of these campaigns.

Literature Review

Primary Data:

For primary data I used actual comment thread that follow the article *I Like It On" Facebook Breast Cancer Campaign Goes Viral* by Ben Parr , blog post *Are 'Save Second Base' breast cancer awareness t-shirts sexist and offensive?* By Rick Chandler, editorial *Breast cancer campaigns demean women* by Beth Bendenhall, and article *'I like it' Facebook status campaign cheapens real cancer fights* by Douglas B. Brill of The Express Times, written in response to the performance of Facebook comments in the "I like it…" breast cancer awareness campaign and other breast cancer awareness campaigns which utilize sexualized language. This actual dialog is real life, real-time, public discourse that is being facilitated by social media.

This data relates to my argument because it documents the debate over whether using sexually charged language is a evidence of what Antonio Gramsci would refer to as "hegemony" at work or what Judith Butler would see as the "reclamation of language". As women (the marginalized group) participate in reinforcing the objectification of their bodies through "I like it on …" breast cancer awareness campaigns in exchange for involving men (who have the power) in the conversation about breast cancer, is the use of this sexually charged language a counter-performance which purposes to re-define the meaning of the words in an effort to reclaim the words and the power they have over women? These dialogs and others like them are the basis of the debate.

Additionally I used information from the National Breast Cancer Awareness Month website to document the history of the fight against breast cancer and suggested strategies that are respectful to women while raising "awareness, education and empowerment."

Secondary Data:

The secondary source materials that I used in this paper are articles which deal with the theoretical framework through which to view this conversation that is unfolding in social media.

First, I discuss the work of Antonio Gramsci in hegemony using the description found in D. Soyin Madison's book *Critical Ethnography*. Madison's version of Gramsci used the term hegemony "to mean, the manner in which dominant classes controlled and exploited subordinate groups by consent, thereby masking exploitation by convincing the exploited that their condition was natural to them, even good for them," (Madison,53).

I also discuss Judith Butlers work on the politics of the performativity as described by Madison. Madison describes Butler's theory of performativity as "a stylized repetition of acts always a reiteration of a norm or set of norms, which means that the act that one does is the act that one performs is, in a sense, an act that has been going on before one arrived on the scene," (Madison, 163). The idea is that others dictate what femaleness is, how females should behave, in a "social construction of femaleness" which one internalizes and believes is "normal" and "natural." This performance includes "speech acts" by which one is "hailed" ("called into being" according to Althusser) or interpellated by society, which may be subverted by "resisting" the "social interpellation" thus "reappropriating" those terms in "counter hegemonic" ways (Butler, *Excitable Speech*).

Additionally I address Phaedra Pezzullo's work on the rhetoric of counter-publics and cultural performance in her *Quarterly Journal of Speech* article, *Resisting "national breast cancer awareness month": the rhetoric of counter publics and their cultural performances* to discuss the role that National Breast Cancer Awareness Month (NBCAM) has in the conversation of breast cancer awareness and the speech acts. According to Pezzullo, the activities of NBCAM have become institutionalized as hegemonic 'common sense measures'….[whose] cultural and medical discourses often promote the business of saving breasts, not lives," (Pezzullo, 344). Pezzullo goes on to say that "The hegemony of patriarchal policies and practices often motivates feminists to respond collectively in hope of altering the conditions and practices of gender-based oppression" through counter publics which "circulate counterdiscourses" which oppose the "oppositional interpretations of their identities, interests and needs," (Pezzullo, 349)

This scholarship relates to this topic because the use of sexual suggestive or "titillating" comments made by women about women's health is shocking, outside the "normative behavior", according to commonly behavior commonly accepted behavior by society for women. By participating in this counterdiscourse women are both subject to the hegemony of sexist language by which society hails them, while at the same time subverting the meaning of the words in an oppositional interpretation of the words in order to gain power in a social discourse.

Finally I discuss Evgeny Morozov's idea of slactivisim found in the conversations over the "I like it on" breast cancer awareness campaigns. According to Morozov, the participation in social media campaigns like the "I like it" campaign can make women feel they have "done something" by posting a comment that "leaves men confused" when in actuality they have not done anything that is of material value to the cause (education, fund raising, research) Morozov's thoughts on slactivism are relevant to this discussion because the "I like it on" breast cancer awareness campaigns have done little more than start a conversation about the campaign. An argument can be (and indeed is) made that women gain power in this process, however there is little material gain for breast cancer awareness or education that results from the campaign.

Introduction:

When one thinks of October three things come to mind, fall, Halloween and National Breast Cancer Awareness Month (NBCAM). Thanks to the tireless efforts of Janelle Hail, breast cancer survivor and founder of the National Breast Cancer Foundation (NBCF), who spread the message that "early detection is the best defense" through education and pink ribbon branding and marketing campaigns which raise funds for breast cancer research, more women than ever have been empowered with knowledge and hope that they can win the battle against breast cancer (NBCF). The efforts to raise awareness about breast cancer have spawned many groups who have joined the fight. Most of these groups spread awareness through respectful means. However there is a growing controversy over those who have harnessed the power of sex to sell and capitalized on the sexualization of breast cancer with "awareness campaigns" that use innuendo and sexually charged speech. An examination of conversations in social media that focus on sexualized breast cancer awareness campaigns reflects public debate that that can be divided into three categories; arguments of hegemony, arguments of counter discourses and arguments of "slactivisim".

National Breast Cancer Awareness Month-The Pinking of America

Breast cancer, two words that strike fear in the heart of a woman because of the deadly force with which the disease strikes its victim and the violence the treatment (often mastectomy) does to her identity as a woman. It is simple enough to define what breast cancer is. The National Breast Cancer Foundation (NBCF) — an organization "committed to spreading knowledge and fostering hope in the fight against breast cancer"— defines cancer as "a disease in which malignant (cancer) cells form in the tissues of the breast". It sounds pretty innocuous, but the devastation the disease leaves in its wake is anything but simple or innocuous. The fight to eradicate breast cancer as the number two cause of death in women in America (lung cancer is number one) (NBCF) has been taken on by organizations like the NBCF through the National Breast Cancer Awareness Month/ Pink Ribbon campaign which encourage "early detection" through a combination of self-exam and regular mammograms. The NBCAM campaign has taken a disease which was once shrouded in the secrecy of taboo and given it a cultural capital as the America turns pink in October to raise awareness for this deadly disease (NBCF).

According to Phaedra Pezzullo, "as the NBCAM has grown exponentially, more people than ever before have begun to talk about breast cancer, a feminist accomplishment in itself." This conversation is a byproduct of what Pezzullo calls the "pinking of America"— the Pink Ribbon campaign started by the NBCF— which employs mass merchandising that markets all things pink to raise awareness and money for "education, research and support"(NBCF).

This is all well and good except that somewhere in the race to eradicate breast cancer the message has shifted from saving the lives of women (and men) who get this deadly disease, which according to the NBCF website will kill 40,000 of the 200,000 women (and men) who are diagnosed annually, to saving breasts because they are sexy(Pezzullo). An example of one of these campaigns is Adam Turman's *Save Second Base* campaign which features t-shirts with a buxom woman in a baseball uniform and the slogan "*Don't let breast cancer steal second base*" (Chandler, 2011). Beth Mendenhall, senior political science and philosophy major at Kansas State University, spoke out about this shift in her *Kansas State Collegian* article *Breast cancer campaigns demean women*, "The new culture of breast cancer awareness can be characterized by two features: appeals to saving the breasts, rather than the women,(sic) and slogans couched in vernacular terms like 'boobs' and 'hooters'" (Mendenhall, 2010). Mendenhall's article sparked a debate among readers in a thread on the college paper's website that went on for nineteen comments.

According to Turman, the proceeds for the $25 t-shirts are donated to Making Strides, an organization that is endorsed by the American Cancer Association (Chandler, 2011). It is Turman's

perspective that a little demeaning slogan is a small price to pay for raising awareness and cash for a deadly

disease.

Breast Cancer Awareness Goes Viral on Facebook

However not all "breast cancer awareness campaigns" are created equal, some campaigns employ

sexist humor without any material contribution to the fight against breast cancer. One such campaign is the

Facebook "I like it" campaign in which women posted status updates like, "I like it on the floor" or "I like it

on the dining room table" (Facebook, *I like it on the floor*), leaving the reader to believe the "it" was sex. The

meme went viral as women posted where they liked "it" as their status and sent this sent message to the

inboxes of all the females on their friend list:

> Remember the game last year about what color bra you were wearing at the moment? The purpose
> was to increase awareness of October Breast Cancer Awareness month. It was a tremendous success
> and we had men wondering for days what was with the colors and it made it to the news. This year's
> game has to do with your handbag/purse, where we put our handbag the moment we get home for
> example "I like it on the couch", "I like it on the kitchen counter", "I like it on the dresser" well u get
> the idea. Just put your answer as your status with nothing more than that and cut n paste this
> message and forward to all your FB female friends to their inbox. The bra game made it to the news.
> Let's see how powerful we women really are!!! REMEMBER – DO NOT PUT YOUR ANSWER
> AS A REPLY TO THIS MESSAGE- PUT IT IN YOUR FACEBOOK STATUS!!! PASS THIS TO
> ALL THE WOMAN YOU KNOW. (Forbes)

According to this message the sexual innuendo of the "game" is used to show women, "how powerful" they

were in leaving, "men wondering for days" women played along in the name of "breast cancer awareness".

Though these "titillating" status updates made the news they did very little material good for the cause of

fighting breast cancer because the creator of the meme failed to include an education component or contact

information for organizations that are engaged in the breast cancer education, research or support. About

the only thing the meme did generate was a contentious debate which played out in the social media

stratosphere.

Hegemony Meets Counterdiscourses

This paper takes a critical look at the debate found in social media over the sexualization of breast cancer awareness campaigns. As one might expect, there are varied responses to these sexualized breast cancer awareness campaigns. Many of the comments amount to high tech name calling and blow-hard bravado. However once the name calling and "nose thumbing" is excluded from the debate three types of arguments are exposed; arguments over hegemony, arguments over slactivism, and arguments over counter-publics performance choices.

One argument that surfaces repeatedly in comment threads is if acceptance of over sexing up breast cancer awareness is if they work. As one commenter put it, This argument follows deeply entrenched hegemonic ideals. D. Soyin Madison addresses Antonio Gramsci's work in hegemony in her book *Critical Ethnography*. Madison defines the term hegemony as "the manner in which dominant classes controlled and exploited subordinate groups by consent, thereby masking exploitation by convincing the exploited that their condition was natural to them, even good for them," (Madison,53). D. Soyin Madison, *Critical Ethnography*.

The debate presents itself as a conflict between those who are convinced that sexing breast cancer awareness is good for the cause and those who object to fundraising at the expense of objectifying women. An example of this conflict can be found in the comment thread following sports writer Rick Chandler's article "Are 'Save Second Base' breast cancer awareness t-shirts sexist and offensive?"

These comments followed the article by Chandler. "It [Save Second Base] will reach more men, which will equal more money for research. Feminist get a grip,"(sasquash20).

Sasquach20's comments drew a response from "fearlessleader", "If it's all right with you guys, we prefer that you show more interest in saving our lives and less interest in your own sexual gratification."

This response from, "phllieshomer" followed, "Men buy funny T-Shirts. It's in our nature."

The response from "sasquash20" and "phillieshomer" follow classic a hegemonic pattern. "Phillieshomer" appeals to the "natural tendency" for men to want "funny t-shirts" (let the reader understand funny to mean that which objectifies women and trivializes breast cancer because it steals the boobies men enjoy). "Sasquash20" also sticks to hegemony's party line as his comment basically conveys the message, 'we men are buying shirts that help you women in the battle against breast cancer, so quit whining over a little objectification.' Both of these commenters are participating in a performance to maintain a hegemonic standard.

Pezzullo believes that "public debates over breast cancer are currently constrained [and] claims that cultural and medial discourses [surrounding breast cancer] often promote the business of 'saving breasts not lives.' A tension exists between the appearance of caring for women and practices that improves women's lives," (Pezzullo, 2003, page 346). "Fearlessleader's" comment engage in a counter-performance which bucks the system as she eloquently states exactly what women want, "show more interest in saving our lives."

The article *Sexing up breast cancer*, by Marry Elizabeth Williams, is a deconstruction of sexualized breast cancer awareness campaigns. This article motivated readers to comment.

"Aargh! It sometimes feels that all the hard work the feminist movement did to bring women's empowerment into focus has been reabsorbed by the consumer culture. Save the Tatas = if you can commodify it you can own it," said DACKS.

DHALGREN responded with a counter suggestion which hints at resignation to hegemonic forces, "It may be necessary to stomach the distasteful marketing aspects in order to promote the worthy end goal," however, she is really involved in a counter-performance as the rest of her comment reveals, "having said that, how does everybody feel about starting a 'Have You Got the Balls?' campaign to raise awareness for testicular cancer?"

Responding in kind "BLACKHAT35" said, "Works for me! [I have] Got a slogan for colorectal cancer. 'Just because you are one doesn't me you have one.'"

In her article, Pezzullo quotes Felski "The experience of discrimination, oppression, and cultural dislocation provides the impetus for the development of a self-consciously oppositional identity," (Pezzullo 2003,349). Pezzullo expands on Felski's thoughts with her own ideas:

> The hegemony of patriarchal policies and practices often motivates feminists to respond collectively in the hopes of altering conditions and practices of gender based oppression... groups invent and circulate counter discourses to formulate oppositional interpretations of their identities, interests, and needs." A counter discourse then, is the rhetorical invention of a discourse that challenges an already existing discourse that has been enabling the oppression of a particular group. (Pezzullo 2003, 349)

"DHALGREN" and "BLACKHATS35" are participating in a "formulating oppositional interpretations of their identities interests and needs" by creating a "counter discourse" in that opposes the "patriarchal policies and practices" of sexist breast cancer awareness campaigns. Their comments take issue directly with hegemony.

In as much as these women may enjoy the idea of objectification of men as a counter performance it is unlikely these slogans that objectify men would garner the same support from females that objectifying women does with males. According to a commenter on *"I Like It On" Facebook Greast cancer Campaign Goes Viral,* Rebecca Mongeon, who's university had a campaign to raise awareness for removing bottle caps from bottles prior to placing them in the recycling receptacles, "called 'Take Your Top Off'....The program (and subsequent posters) generated a lot of attention and planted that idea into people's minds" (Parr). This performance choice objectifies women defying the social norm of not going topless in public. Building on the success of sexual innuendo from the "Take Your Top Off' campaign, the next campaign objectified males to raise awareness of students carbon footprint, "'How Big is Your Package' which was found to be a little excessive in the innuendo," (Parr).

Performance of Oppositional Interpretation or Slactivist Showmanship

There are other ways to engage in counter discourses which take the meaning of the sexist comments and use them to empower group members through "reclamation" of language. For Judith Butler, reclaimation of language occurs when marginalized groups engage in behavior or speech outside the "normative behavior", according to commonly accepted standards for societal behavior they are participating in counterdiscourses. By participating in this counterdiscourse in these cases women are both subject to the hegemony of sexist language by which society hails them [Althusser's theory of being called into being], while at the same time subverting the meaning of the words in an "oppositional interpretation" of the words in order to gain power in a social discourse.

The Facebook "I like it" campaign was an attempt at this idea of oppositional interpretation. Women circulated messages to the women on their friend lists asking them to post status updates which contained sexual innuendo in an effort to confuse men and exert power over them by pointing out their "natural" sexual bent. The message indicated that when the meme took off it would receive media coverage and thus obtain a platform for a conversation about breast cancer. Unfortunately neither the Facebook message circulated (Forbes) nor the Facebook web page contained any information on breast cancer or the contact information which would facilitate an individual donation (I like it on the floor, Facebook).

However, many of the comments following articles about the viral meme simply found this campaign to be a weak attempt at activism. Evgeny Morozov talks about this non-activisim activisim in his book *The Net Delusion: The Darker Side of Internet Freedom*. Morozov has a special term for this phenomenon, "slactivism". According to Morozov, "The problem with political activism facilitated by social networking sites is that much of it happens for reasons that have nothing to do with one's commitment to ideas and politics in general, but rather to impress one's friends," (Morozov,186). Morozov also criticizes online activism which is accomplished with the click of a mouse or the posting of a status because, "when communications costs are low, groups can easily spring into action," (Morozov, 180). Morozov accuses these pseudo-participants involve themselves in the "shallow" activity of a "narcissistic" society which looks involved without moving away from their seat in front of the computer (Morozov, 186-187).

Many people, like Adam Richtar, present arguments that agree with Morozov's criticism. Richtar posted a comment in response to Douglas Brill's article on the Lehigh Valley Live website, "Changing your Facebook status takes no effort and costs you nothing. Better to go out and do something constructive and fight against breast cancer," (Brill, lehighvalleylive.com).

Aj, responded in agreement, "I personally think this is a stupid idea mainly because I'm a guy and I didn't think perverted about it because that doesn't seem likely that a bunch of females would do such a thing." Aj, didn't believe that the women he knew would deliberately post such lewd comments under 'normal' circumstances. Something was up. Aj went on to say, "Plus if someone doesn't know something they just search it up on Google like I did…..good job leaving us in the dark ladies…... maybe someday your gender will be as smart as it claims to be." Not only was Aj not duped (as women hoped he would be) he also subverted the "ladies" subversive use of language (the only way to get men interested in breast cancer awareness is by piquing their sexual awareness) and infantile treatment of his sex (pun intended).

Some argued that the campaign was effective. Ashleigh Graf of the Express-Times commented, "But it seems to be doing exactly what its purpose was meant to be: raising awareness of breast cancer. Would you ever have written a blog about Breast Cancer Awareness Month if not for this viral movement?" Graf puts a point on it when she points out that Douglas a male in the class of oppressor who has been duped into writing a blog on Breast Cancer Awareness which he might not otherwise have written had it not been for women's Facebook performance. B Thomas supports Graff, "The whole point was to gain media coverage and therefore awareness of breast cancer, not money."

Conclusion:

The debate over the best way to "raise awareness" for breast cancer involves many complex issues which revolve around the of use of language as a means of oppression or as a method of freedom. An examination of conversations in social media that focus on sexualized breast cancer awareness campaigns reflects public debate that will not be resolved in the near future. These debates which pit hegemony against counter discourses and debate oppositional interpretation versus "slactivism" will continue to play themselves out in social media where more and more people will join the conversation.

Commenter, Karen Rose, had a great idea that combines counterdiscourse with a breast cancer educational component that I think is far more effective than the Facebook "I like It" lewd cryptic status updates, "Personally I don't see the connection between purses and breast cancer. I'm encouraging my friends to post the date of their last clinical breast exam or mammogram. 'The last time I did it was on (date).' Same 'shock' factor, but better tied to breast cancer awareness. BTW….I am planning on doing it next month.:)"(Parr, 15) In her comment, Rose also included a link to a non-profit cancer group where readers could get information or get involved.

I agree with Rose that "When I post the date of my last exam it does a couple of important things. First it reminds me to schedule my next one of it's been a while. Second it allows women who haven't scheduled an exam to see that it's not anything to be afraid of because their friends have done it," (Parr, 16) In the end I think that the measure of success or failure of the sexualized "breast cancer awareness" campaigns can only be quantified in increasing "empowerment" for women. In order for a counterdiscourse to be effectively empower women the counterdiscourses must subvert *meaning* of the words that it purports to change and while sexualized "breast cancer awareness" campaigns may raise awareness (and funds) because they reinforce deeply entrenched hegemonic ideals which objectify women and trivialize women's health they do not raise the value (level of respect) for women which makes them a failure.

5 COMPUTERIZED BABIES

By
Courtney Tarrillion

Introduction

We, as a society, are at a point where technology is capable of doing amazing things. We can turn our vehicles on by remote control, have our cell-phones perform voice commands for us, video-chat with people across the world, and so much more. The problem isn't with all of this advancement though, it is with our comfort level with this advancement. We are coming up with robots and various forms of technology for basically everything that we as humans have to do.

At some point though, don't we have to question whether these acts are something we shouldn't leave up to technology or robots to do, and that we should be doing ourselves? I would argue that there is, or should be some kind of line drawn as to what things are "sacred" and shouldn't be performed by anything other than humans. For example, care taker robots are being created to take care of elderly people or young children, but is this ethical? Should we leave the care of our loved ones in the hands of a machine? Furthermore, what is it saying about us as a culture if we start handing off our elderly to robotic machine care takers? I know that I wouldn't want to be taken care of by a robot, simply because I had gotten older. And in the case of children, it seems highly inappropriate and wrong to be leaving the raising of a human being in the "hands" of someone/thing who isn't even a human being. Child rearing should be a scared and treasured thing among humans, and so I argue that it should be left up to the actual humans themselves.

What kind of further generations will we have if everyone is brought up by robot "parent" figures? Because of this, I think it is important to look into human relationships and attachments on technology, and to decide now what is and isn't acceptable behavior. If we decide ahead of time what forms of attachment are alright than we bypass the notion of one day having to correct things , because the relationships have gotten out of hand and have somehow crossed a line of what is acceptable behavior. We need to determine what behaviors are acceptable between humans and robots before these preformed behaviors start to take away from our own humanity and lessen the value of human to human contract and interaction.

Literature Review

Recently the technology of Real Care Babies has become quite a popular technology to use for educational purposes. It is a helpful tool used in many schools that aims to educate (mostly) teens on what it is like to be responsible for and take care of a baby in the hopes that this will prevent them from having children of their own at a young age. Since this is a relatively new technology, not much research has been done on the subject and so there is little information on the topic other than how effective people think it may or may not be. Somers article is one of the few scholarly articles that studies the effectiveness of the Baby Think it over program. Much of the study deals with "white, middle class, suburban high school students," most of whom were females. The study recognized that this was a very specific group and acknowledged a desire to see how things would have been with a variety of races and more male participants. The Baby Think it Over website as well as the Real Care Baby website were both helpful tools in learning more about the technology that I am dealing with and provided necessary information as to how these Real care babies actually operate.

Since there already isn't much information done on Robotic babies, it was important to reach out and look into related fields, like that of robotic pets. A significant amount of research has been done on robotic pets and how they both contribute to our world and make us question their ethical role. The Fischman article discussed research done at the University of Missouri in Columbia where they found stress levels were reduced in participants with robotic pets. Similarly the Watts article found that elderly robotic pet owners were found to be less lonely and that the robotic pets had a very positive impact on their lives. Other researchers like McNicol and Nambo looked into the therapeutic aspects that the robotic pets could and did in fact offer. Continued research by Johnson, and Takanori indicated that these robotic pets were capable of adapting to what their owners desired from them. In some cases the robotic pets were even described as taking on a personality of their own.

The next section of my research went into dealing with adolescents and technology. Many of the articles discussed the importance of educating young people about technology and the proper way to use it. Some would argue that this isn't actually being done though, and that much of our youth has no idea about what the "proper" use of technology is, and what is acceptable or not. In their defense, this is partly due to the fact that we, as a culture, haven't exactly determined what this is or not. Much of what I am questioning is in fact that we haven't decided what behaviors are acceptable with technology, specifically robots, but it seems like this is a necessary thing to do ahead of time, before things get out of hand and it's too little, too late.

I also did a small amount of research on the new i-phone program, Siri, to use as another robotic device that many people are coming into contact with now. This technology is so new though that there hasn't even been enough time to do any research on it yet. The apple website was about the best place to find out anything about the device, but that is about it. I really think that this is going to be an important field of study though in the future, once more time has passed and more people have this specific device.

Overall each of the articles were helpful in gathering information for my topic. It was important to get varying viewpoints on technology and see how there are both positive and negative aspects when dealing with robots and robotic devices. The most important thing to remember to me, is how new all of this information is and how any research done on it is significant and groundbreaking, because it really is the first of its kind. I'm positive that much more research will be done on this area in the future, but for now we have to sort of pick pieces from various areas, and scrap up what we can in order to draw any sort of conclusion.

Methods

The overall premise of my project requires me to look at a series of YouTube videos in order to analyze how humans are reacting towards and treating robot babies. In my initial research I was questioning human interaction with technology. After researching the "Real care babies" and the "baby think it over" program, I was more interested in studying the relationship between humans and robots; a more specific form of technology.

I don't personally know anyone who currently has a real care baby, and so I couldn't study this behavior live, but thankfully because of how advanced our world really is, I could watch video journals where students documented what it was like to have a real care baby. Through these videos I interpreted their body language and voice changes as well as their behaviors to get a good idea on the information I needed. Since there are plenty of videos out there, I tried to pick varying races and genders as well as socio-economic classes to see if this information played a role in how attached the teenagers became.

Once I had chosen all the videos I wanted to use, I would then watch each one more thoroughly and transcribe it into text form, so that it could be further interpreted and analyzed, as well as quoted throughout my research. The video journal entries are roughly between three and twelve minutes long and detail what it is like to have and take care of a Real Care Baby.

Some of the videos have been edited to include background music, introduction slides, closing credits, etc, while others are very basic start to finish without any extra work done to them. I could have chosen really any of the videos out there, but I figured there needed to be some kind of order and reasoning behind the individuals selected for my project. Because of this, I tried to select members from both sexes, as well as varying ethnicities. This was much easier to do for the girls than it was for the boys. There aren't nearly as many male participants in this area as female participants, so it was difficult to find them at all, let alone chose them based on race. I was able to locate videos of female participants who were Caucasian, Hispanic, African American, and Asian, while all of the male participants were from one ethnicity; Caucasian.

Watching video entries makes my ethnography project much different than some others. While on one hand you could argue that I am truly able to see these participants in their natural state, because they aren't altering their behavior based on who is around and watching them, on the other hand the mere fact that they are being recorded could be changing the way they behave. In addition to this, I am unable to interview my participants and ask them further questions than what is being answered onscreen. Much of my research has to come from what I believe is reasonable to draw from the data that I have gathered.

As with any ethnography, ethics is always questioned. With my research the question is focused towards the ethics of studying adolescents. Usually you need all kinds of permission forms and waivers in order to observe minors, but because I am not directly viewing minors, and am instead watching video journal entries produced by these individuals, this matter is not handled in the same way. Many would argue that there are still parts of the research that they are uncomfortable with, since the participants are unaware that they are a part of my data, but after attending the academic Krost symposium this year, I am more than aware that once something is up on the Internet, you don't have much control over it anymore, regardless of your age.

A small portion of my project focused on the use of the new i-phone program Siri. This program is so new that nothing other than the information page on the apple website was really available as research on this area. I wanted to interview people on how they felt having the Siri program on their i-phones, but it was difficult at the time to find people who had this program and were willing to let me interview them. Because of this I was only able to get two interviews from people about Siri, which I then transcribed into text form.

At the very beginning of my research, I handed out a very general survey to less than fifty people to get an idea of how to begin my project and what questions I should be asking as a way to gather information and have a sort of starting place. The original idea was to pair these finding with the Siri interviews and have a whole other section on robotic technology to go along with the massive amount of data I now have on the Real care Babies. I know that in the future this will be a popular and important area of study, but at this point there isn't enough information to go off of and the subject matter just wasn't meshing well with the data I was gathering already from the rest of my project.

Once I had done each of these things, I was able to really zone in on what area I wanted my project to focus on, and was then able to go into much more detail than I originally thought on the Real Care Babies portion. These area is so new and original that it really needed its own project anyways and was more than capable of standing alone, while still recognizing the existence of other robotic devices that humans are coming into contact with just as often if not more so.

Analysis

There are many ways in which humans interact with technology. Instead of reading hard-cover books, we can download the pages onto our hand held devices and read them from screens, instead of checking out at a grocery store with a human cashier, we can go through self check-out, and instead of showing our ID's to security guards in order to enter a building, we can now use magnetic key cards. Every day new technologies are being programmed to aid humans in some way, one of these technologies is that of Real Care Babies. Real Care Babies are small robots aimed to imitate human children and serve the purpose of educating people on what it is like to be responsible for and care for a child.

What exactly is a computerized baby?? Computerized Babies are basically robots fashioned into the shape and size of a human infant. They are covered with soft plastic and made to feel and look as close to a real baby as possible. Each "baby" has sensors throughout its body to detect if it is being properly cared and attended. For example; there is a sensor on its mouth as well as one on the provided bottle so the computer within the baby can record how long it cried before the bottle sensor touched the mouth sensor, and how long it was kept there for. If the bottle is taken away before the baby is "done" then it will continue to cry.

The "babies" are programmed to be cared for very similar to a living child. They require head support, bottle feeding, burping, diaper changes, and tending to, and "just like a real baby they cry at all hours of the day or night". The main program using this technology is *"Baby think it Over"* with the *"Real Care Baby"*. This program uses the robotic babies to teach people (mostly teenagers) what it is like to care for a baby 24/7.

You cannot simply turn the baby off nor can you give it away to someone else to "babysit". The key is attached to a medical bracelet which is placed on the care givers wrist when they check out the baby. This bracelet cannot be taken off and if it is cut off the baby will cry continuously until it is turned back on. The key on the bracelet is essential to the care of the baby, because it must be inserted into the back of the child to signal to the computer that the child is indeed being cared for by the person who checked it out. This measure was put into place to force the caregiver to really know what it's like to have a child and not be able to just give it away to someone when things get difficult. (Note: the Real Care Baby II doesn't require a key, but registers when the bracelets sensor touches it.)

In one video a teenage girl tells how awful her night was with the Real Care baby waking her up so often, but then she completely flips and says that it wasn't that frustrating and she actually had fun. Then she lovingly calls it "my baby" and touches it on the stomach indicating an affection towards the robot child. She goes on to say "it was nice waking up and having a baby to take care of" but adds in "let's see how I feel after a few more days" (she had the baby during a holiday weekend, so longer than most participants). These observations bring up my next point, on what other affects the computerized babies are having on these adolescents. It's true that they are an ingenious invention, aimed at helping to prevent teenage pregnancy by showing young people what it's truly like to be responsible for a baby, but are there any negative aspects?

After studying the research on the use of computerized animals and pet robots, (Turkle) I would argue that a bond is formed between the "owner/ caregiver" and the robot, and I would question whether this is an appropriate relationship or not. Yes, the robots are suppose to teach people what it is like to take care of a child, but are we suppose to feel towards this robotic baby the way we would feel towards a human child? Why do we care if the robotic baby is comfortable or not, or if it is "hungry" or "tired" or "needs to be changed"? Should we be treating a robot like a human and caring as much for it as we would any other child? Arguably, all of these questions remain unanswered, and it is unclear what should be done. Since robotic pets and babies are a relatively new concept, there isn't much research done on the after effects of having one for an extended period of time. Most people will tell you about how they learned something about responsibility, but is anyone asking if they developed feelings towards the baby, or if they miss it, or didn't want to give it back? And if these things are true, what is to be done? How should we respond to humans forming relationships with robots?

In another diary video, a teenage boy seemed to grow rather attached to his "baby boy", who he named Caden. He started the weekend with the baby not really caring overly for it, but as the clips went on you could see a definite growth in the way he felt about the "baby". In the last scene the teenager is seen lying in bed with the baby's head resting on his arm sleeping. The teenage boy questions to the camera "is it weird that we are sleeping together?" and then goes on to say he can't wait to have a baby of his own one day and that having Caden wasn't as hard as everyone told him it was going to be. He even mentions to the camera that he is going to miss the robotic baby "Caden" and writes this statement again in the closing credits.

This boy acknowledges the fact that he has feelings for this robot baby. He will miss not having it around in the same sense that he would miss another human being. These bonds seem innocent enough, but that brings up the question of when do we draw the line? What kind of relationship between human and robot/ technology is no longer appropriate and who determines that? Furthermore, who would enforce that? Does it not seem odd to anyone else that this teenage boy is going to miss having a robotic baby waking him up at all hours of the night? Another questioning thought that was brought to mind after this video was on the effectiveness of the Real Care Babies. If this boy says he can't wait to have a baby of his own and that it wasn't nearly as hard as he thought it was going to be, then doesn't that in fact provoke the opposite ideas that the Real Care Babies are trying to install in young people. The Real Care Babies are supposed to teach teenagers (and others) how difficult it can be to be fully responsible for another life and how much they have to give up in order to care about someone else above themselves.

The program wants young people to realize they aren't ready to be parents yet and should wait to have sex until they are in fact ready to take on this responsibility. Is this the outcome gained for this teenage boy though? I would argue that it is not... He doesn't want to turn the baby back in, he wants to have a baby of his own, and he doesn't think taking care of the baby was that hard.

I thought it was interesting that most of the quotes used on the actual "*Real Care Baby*" site or "*Baby Think it Over*" site are positive responses to the program on how they are not ready to have children yet, while most of the random journal entries and video diaries show contrast to this. Regardless of whether they say they are ready to have kids or not, they are treating this robots like they would treat a real life infant and list how they will miss not having the baby around to take care of, and how it was nice having something who "needs you". Obviously these babies don't actually need anyone though. They may cry, or rather sound like they are crying, but the robots are in no danger if not taken care of by someone. It's interesting to note how easily it seems that people are able to form these close connections to their *Real Care Baby*.

After observing members from varying ethnicities, I came to the conclusion that race did not seem to be a factor in determining a subjects likely-hood of becoming attached to the robotic babies or not. There were signs from every video, regardless of race, that would suggest the participants formed a connection with these Real Care Babies. For example; using a "baby voice" was present in every video journal that I observed. What I mean by a "baby voice" is that high pitch, cooing sort of speech that people tend to use when they are talking to babies. Participant one with Baby Caden, uses multiple examples of this when he says things like "little bitty toes", "who's a good baby", and "good boy".

Gender also didn't seem to be a determinate either, as both males and females became attached to their Real Care Babies at least to some degree. In fact I would argue that given the transcripts from each video journal, without identification of what gender they belong to, most people wouldn't be able to determine if the participant was male or female. Both sexes had examples of participants kissing their babies on the forehead, using baby talk, and affectionately caressing the Real Care Babies.

Only two of the participants switched between using vocabulary like "it/its" to "he/she/his/hers" while the others almost always, or did always use "he/she/his/hers" gender specific terminology. I thought this point was interesting to note because by identifying the gender of the baby they are giving it human qualities. All of the participants did at one point, identify the gender of their baby and use terminology like "he/she/his/hers" and no one continually referred to their baby as "it".

It seems important to categorize the ways in which these teens are humanizing these Real Care Babies. First, they chose whether there baby is a boy or girl, so now they can say "good boy" or "little girl", etc. Second, they further the humanization of these robotic babies by giving them names. In transcript six the male participant continually refers to his baby as "it", until the point at which his mother asks him "what's her name?" At this point the baby has been identified as a girl and so the male participant starts referring to his baby as "she, her". Another important thing to note here, is the role of the parent; the mother is the one who influences her son into humanizing the baby and referring to it as a girl, and could show how some of these behaviors are perhaps taught by parental figures. Thirdly, these babies are given diapers and clothes as yet another example of how a robot is being humanized. In transcript six again; the mother says "Her old diaper, she doesn't even get clothes or anything, she gets one outfit?" like this is some huge shock. But why is this shocking? Robots don't need clothes, and they certainly don't need more than one outfit, but humans do, or at least we are expected to have more than one outfit. So, wouldn't the fact that we are unhappy with the thought of a robotic baby only having one outfit, show how we have humanized the baby in a way that raises it value to that of our own, or close to?

In cases where the participant seemed to be alone and no one else was seen or heard in the video, they were more likely to show a connection to the Real care Baby. Examples of this include more "baby talk", lying down holding their baby, cooing at the baby, caressing the baby, and more playing with the baby. While we can only speculate, it seems reasonable to assume that the teens who are home alone, or by themselves are more likely to be looking for that human to human interaction, and are therefore more likely to connect with the Real Care Baby, especially once it has been at least partially humanized already.

In transcript one the participant is never seen with anyone else while he is at his house and we never hear anyone else in the background either. He seems to be one of the participants who grows the most attached to his Real Care baby and even says he "can't wait to actually have one of (his) own" and that he will "miss Caden", his Real Care Baby. He is also one of the participants who regularly kisses his Real Care Baby on the forehead and speaks to it like a human baby, with "baby talk".

He isn't the only example of this though, in transcript four the participant also seems to be completely alone and she too, seems to become rather attached to her baby. At one point she films herself stroking the baby while saying "my baby" in the "baby talk voice" as well. She also starts off by saying how frustrating the experience has been, but then later on says "it wasn't really that frustrating or like annoying, it was actually really fun". This statement seems to be entirely contradictory since her exact words earlier on in the video were, "I was so frustrated".

So why would she contradict herself like this, and what does that show? To me this shows, on an extended level, her attachment to this Real Care Baby. Human children often frustrate us, but we still love them and forgive them and move on, because they are just children, so it seems like this participant is treating her Real Care Baby just as we treat human children, by moving on from the upsetting parts about the baby and still caring for it.

Another interesting thing to point out is that all but one of the video participants I observed referred to themselves as "mommy" or "daddy" at least once. In transcript one the participant tells his Real Care Baby "I love you Caden" and then uses his own voice to speak for the baby and says "I love you more Daddy". In transcript two the participant says "yeah, let mommy sleep." In transcript five the female participant refers to herself as having "mommy-hair", etc. These teenagers are taking care of robotic babies for a weekend and yet they are already attached enough to where they are referring to themselves as either "mommy" or "daddy".

Earlier I brought up the connection between robotic pets and these robotic babies. Since not much research has been done with the Real Care babies, I was able to find information of a similar area; Robotic pets. These robots are made to look like dogs, cats and other animals and have been used in multiple studies including one done with elderly people where they found that the robotic pets were a comforting tool in these peoples' lives. The robotic pets seemed real enough to be able to aid these elderly folks into feeling less alone, and more cared for. The "pets" had high results in decreasing feeling of loneliness and depression and these older people grew quite attached to them, in the same manner they would to a real living pet. (Fischman)

Just as with the robotic pets, these Real Care Babies seem to be providing some kind of companionship for some of these teenagers, especially the ones who seem to be alone throughout their video journal entries. It would seem reasonable to assume that just as these robotic pets made elderly people feel less lonely and depressed, the same may be true with many of these teenagers and their robotic babies. At least two of them said something along the lines of how it was nice to have someone to wake up to. It seems like they feel better about themselves by thinking that someone(thing) needs them, even if it is a robotic baby.

Just as discussed in Sherry Turkles book, *Alone Together*, we have to step back and look at our relationship with technology. Each individual step may seem like no big deal, but what is going to happen in the long run? Yah it may seem fine to sleep with your phone next to your bed, but it's not that far of a jump to actually having to be touching your phone to fall asleep, which most people would see as borderline crossing the line on how intimate we should be with an inanimate object. Yes, robots serve hugely helpful in our everyday lives and tasks, and we have become quite accustomed to having things be so simple for us, but how do we know when we have to do something ourselves? When is it no longer appropriate to have assistance or help on something, or with something from a robot or some other form of technology? Turkle demonstrates that humans come to care for what they nurture, and because of this I would argue that by asking teens to care for computerized babies, we are encouraging them to build a nurturing relationship with robots and non-living things.

There are just so many ways that technology like this can grow, especially now that the computerized babies are available to the public and can be purchased online. I'm sure there are a lot of situations one could come up with.. let's say, for example, that a woman cannot have children and decided to purchase one of these robot babies to have in place of her own child. Is this an okay use for the babies? Would it be more okay if it was just for a matter of months versus years?? Would that even make a difference? If teenagers who don't even want kids are finding themselves becoming easily attached to these robotic babies after only a weekend, then imagine how a female who can't have children of her own might feel towards the computerized baby.

With so many orphaned children in the world I worry about the impact robotic babies could have. It seems highly problematic that one day these Real Care Babies could serve as a substitute for couples or individually who can't have children of their own. In this instance I would say that these robotic babies are taking away chances from actual babies and therefore having a negative impact on us as humans. This is all very hypothetical and futuristic, but seems like a valid point to be considering before it's too late.

As I mentioned before it seems as though this program isn't working exactly as they probably expected.

These teenagers don't seem like they are completely appalled by the idea of having a child at such a young age, and in fact it seems like this program made many of them even more excited to have kids. It is important to note that some good is still coming from this program though. In many cases it seems like this program has taught its participants compassion and put them in touch with their nurturing side. These teenagers do know what it's like to be fully responsible for a child now, even if they didn't think it was very hard.

Conclusion

At some point a connection with robots has to in fact, put into question our own humanity. It is at this point that the relationship has crossed some kind of line and needs to be reevaluated. Humanizing robotic babies may seem innocent enough to some at this time, but without guidelines who knows how this relationship could develop and change. We need to determine what behaviors are acceptable between humans and robots before these preformed behaviors start to take away from our own humanity and lessen the value of human to human contract and interaction.

Because of this, it seems fair to at least recognize that there is a potential for risk with these robotic babies, no matter how beneficial they also are. You have been left with a lot of questions, simply because there aren't too many answers at this point. The technology of robots is fairly new and still advancing so it's hard to perceive where things are going. The Real Care Babies are an intelligent and useful tool for young adults and should continue to be used, I just simply want people to question their individual relationships with machines/ robots and technology. You may not even realize you have a relationship with technology and its devices, but you do. This is the time when we need to decide what level of a relationship is acceptable with technology before all the small steps build up, and we are left with a situation in which we feel that our own humanity has been devalued, because of a connection with these robots.

Annotated Bibliography:

Fischman, Josh. "A Healthy Little Robot" U.S. News & World Report; 12/12/2005,   Vol. 139
Issue 22, p74-74, 1p, 1 Color Photograph

This was a study done at the University of Missouri in Columbia where they studied peoples stress
levels before and while petting a robotic pet. They found that stress levels declined while interacting with
the robot pet and that when the robot dog was sent to elderly people they were found to be less lonely or
depressed.

Johnson, Steven. "Smart Robot Pet Tricks". Discover; Feb2004, Vol. 25 Issue 2,   p26-27, 2p, 1 Color
Photograph

This article examined the idea of a robotic dog taking on its own personality. The dog was programmed
in such a way where it would develop based on what its owners want from it not to mention that the dog
could just download new data and be programmed to behave a certain way, giving it some resemblance of a
personality.

McNicol, Tony. "A Robopet Revolution". J@pan Inc.; Dec2003, Issue 50, p40-46, 7p, 11 Color
Photographs

This article takes a look at the idea of having a robotic pet provide some kind of comfort to its owners.
It discusses the idea of Japan becoming a dog loving country and how AIBO took that idea and created a
robotic dog for the people of Japan.

Nambo, Hidetaka. "Implementation of owner distinction for therapeutic pet robots. Electrical Engineering
in Japan; Oct2009, Vol. 169 Issue 1, p20-27, 8p

This article channels the idea of incorporating pet robots into therapeutic animal assisted therapy.

*Patton, Kim. "Teens And Technology." Young Adult Library Services 9.2 (2011): 3. Academic Search Complete.
Web. 9 Jan. 2012.

This was a short article discussing the idea and dangers of teenagers and technology. It is important for
us to educate these teenagers on "their rights and responsibilities" when it comes to using technology as well
as the risks and things to avoid. The article also briefly touches on cyber-bullying, sexting, and illegal file
sharing.

*Skinner, D., et al. "Evaluation of Use of Cell-phones To Aid Compliance With Drug Therapy For HIV
Patients." AIDS care 19.5 (2007): 605-607. Academic Search Complete. Web. 9 Jan 2012.

I'm not sure how relevant this article is to my project any more, but originally I thought it was
interesting to note all the things that we can now do from and with our phones. This article is all about the
benefits of using a cell phone during therapy for HIV patients.

*Somers, Cheryl L., and Mariane M. Fahlman. "Effectiveness of the "Baby Think it Over" Teen Pregnancy Prevention Program." *Journal of School Health* 71.5 (2001): 188 *Academic Search Complete*. Web. 9 Jan. 2012

This is one of the few scholarly articles that studies the effectiveness of the Baby Think it over program. Much of the study deals with "white, middle class, suburban high school students," most of whom were females. The study recognized that this was a very specific group and acknowledged a desire to see how think would have been with a variety of races and more male participants.

*Takanori Shibata, et al. "Interactive Pet Robot With An Emotion Model." *Advanced Robotics* 13.3 (1999): 225. *Academic Search Complete*. Web. 9 Jan. 2012.

This article looks into the idea of an interactive pet robot. It would be able to "form" a personality and adapt to behaviors that its owner deems positive.

Unlisted. "Computerized Babies". Indian Life; Jan/Feb2001, Vol. 21 Issue 4, p3, 2p, 1 Black and White Photograph

This article reports the development of computerized babies as a learning tool and how they can be used to their full advantage. It also references them as a more current parenting tool.

*Watts, Jonathan. "Toy Cat Companion For Elderly Is Unveiled." *Lancet* 353.9159 (1999): 1166. *Academic Search Complete*. Web. 9 Jan. 2012

In this article the idea of pet robots in brought into play as being companions to elderly people. Many studies have shown that the presence of a pet (even a robotic one) helps improve the well being of the elderly.

*Zhou Changjiu, et al. "False Alarm Metrics For Human-Robot Interactions in Service Robots." *Advanced Robotics* 24.13 (2010): 1841-1859. *Academic Search Complete*. Web. 9 Jan. 2012

This study was done because of the increased interest lately in service robots. A lot of ethical questions seem to arise from this article in interpreting the justness of "service robots". This was a rather in depth study that went into a lot of detail on the safety and makeup of these robots.

*http://www.apple.com/iphone/features/siri-faq.html

Since Siri is so new, there hasn't been enough time for many articles to be produced on the matter. This is the official Apple page for Siri and was really helpful in understand what Siri is and what it's capable of.

*http://unews.com/2011/09/26/when-technology-goes-too-far/

This university article discusses the fine line of when technology has "gone too far". What are we alright with? and when is it suddenly too much for us to handle and be ok with?

*http://www.helium.com/items/1786360-when-technology-goes-too-far

This article also discusses the idea of technology "going too far". Many examples are listed and questions are raised within this piece of work.

Informational Websites:

*_Baby think it over_ Website:

http://www.timolson.com/babythink.htm#The

*_Real Care Baby_ Website:

http://www.realityworks.com/infantsimulations/realcarebaby.asp

Video Journal Entries:

*Youtube.com Baby think it over Diary accounts:

Krost References:

Turkle, Sherry. _Alone Together; Why we expect more from Technology and less from each other_, Basic Books, 2011. New York.

Methods References:

Farrington-Darby, T., & Wilson, J. R. (2009). Understanding social interactions in complex work: a video ethnography. _Cognition, Technology & Work_, _11_(1), 1-15. doi:10.1007/s10111-008-0118-z

Hemmings, Annette. Ethnographic Research with Adolescent Students: Situated Fieldwork Ethics and Ethical Principles Governing Human Research (2008) _Journal of Empirical Research on Human Research Ethics._ (27-38)

Li, Jun. Ethical Challenges in Participant Observation: A Reflection on Ethnographic Fieldwork. *The Qualitative Report* Volume 13, Number 1, March 2008, 100-115

http://www.nova.edu/ssss/QR/QR13-1/li.pdf

MacLure, M., Holmes, R., MacRae, C., & Jones, L. (2010). Animating classroom ethnography: overcoming video-fear. *International Journal Of Qualitative Studies In Education (QSE)*, *23*(5), 543-556. doi:10.1080/09518391003645370

Watras, Joseph. ETHNOGRAPHY AND ETHICS: A CRITIQUE OF GREGORY BATESON (1904-1980). (2010). *Journal of Ethnographic & Qualitative Research*, *5*(2), 127-137.

6 EVENING THE PLAYING FIELD: How social media changes the dynamic between

fan and athlete

By
Brandon Boylan

"It should be fun. That is what I try to do, just keep it fun. People look to guys like us to be positive

and fun, and that's where I try to keep the focus. Make people want to come back because they have fun

with the interaction" (Deveney, 2010, p.22)

Those are the words of Dwight Howard on what he thinks about the ability of athletes to communicate

directly with fans via social media. His words encompass what comes through this new wave of

communication. Fan and athlete both gain something and want to participate in the interaction.

This paper will delve deeper into what those words touch on showing that the ability of the two parties

to interact like never before has impacted sports, creating a relationship between two groups previously

living in separate spheres.

BACKGROUND ON FAN AND ATHLETE INTERACTION

Before really being able to dig into the nature of the new relationship within sports, it is important to

understand the traditional interaction between fans and athletes. This is defined as a parasocial relationship,

defined as "one-sided interpersonal relationships that 'television viewers establish' with media characters'"(Sun, 2010, p.196).

Parasocial relationships are a part of sports because, in large, fans experience sports via a television or computer screen. While attending a game there is a barrier between the players and the fans. Therefore, fans have reason for creating a parasocial relationship with certain athletes, as "it is likely that fans develop parasocial relationships with athletes who play on the same team" (p.197). Still, fans "tended to connect more with their favorite athletes than to their favorite team" because "for sports fans, athletes look more personal and tangible than teams" (p. 208). Like a media character matters to a viewer, so does an individual athlete.

These relationships are one sided because only the viewer, in this case the fan, is building the relationship and causing the connection. For the most part, viewers establish relationships with the people they see on television with whom they identify because "parasocial relationships (have) also been found to depend on the media character's looks, behavior, humor, speech characteristics, emotional state and nonverbal behavior" (p. 196). Fans bond with an athlete because they see bits of themselves.

Now there has been a shift from this completely parasocial, separated relationship. Social media allows for communication to occur between groups previously brought together only by games, special events, autograph signings or the traditional media. This capability is redefining what the relationship between fan and athlete really is.

The connection can be seen in the blog maintained by Curt Schilling, a now retired baseball pitcher who established folklore status with the Boston Red Sox by playing with an injured, and bloody, ankle to help the Red Sox beat the rival Yankees and eventually win the World Series. In a working-class town like Boston, where the people are deeply connected to their team, the workhorse approach of Schilling became legend. But Schilling began to connect with the fans on a personal level through his blog, 38pitches.com. On the blog, Schilling created a connection with fans and reciprocally "support was generated from blog readers, who mobilized as a collective support group for Schilling" on topics ranging from the "bloody sock" and steroid use in baseball to sports journalists (Sanderson, 2010, p. 201). Schilling used his blog to reach out to the fans directly and thus "become empowered to bypass traditional reporting channels" (p.201). Will Leitch of *The Sporting News* points out that social media has created a way for players to "speak directly to the fans" (2008, p. 15).

Prior to social media, the only way that a player could talk directly to a fan was through an organized event, like a season ticket holder dinner or an autograph signing. There was never any deep knowing of the person because such a forum is limited by time, the mass of people attending and the social norms that make such events more for formalities then personalities. Other than such events, fans could only know athletes through their athletic performances, how they presented themselves in press conferences and/or how the athlete was presented in the traditional media. In sum, there was very much a barrier between the two groups.

Leitch explains, "it's little wonder that athletes, buoyed by technology, are taking back the power" to report about themselves for themselves because it allows for them to directly represent themselves before fans (2008, p. 15). One of the most proactive athletes was Chris Bosh, a basketball player now of the Miami Heat. When with the Toronto Raptors, Bosh was known as a great player, but in terms of commercial marketability he was not on the level of Shaquille O'Neal, Dwight Howard or Dwayne Wade. Therefore, he worked to promote himself on YouTube when, in 2008, he became the first athlete to try and gain All-Star votes from fans by creating humorous videos of himself "in the style of a relentless used-car salesman" (Deveney, 2010, p. 22). The video, viewed over 700,000 times, "would be seminal for Bosh and other athletes" because it showed that people were interested in the personality of athletes and thus "opened a floodgate, demonstrating an opportunity for players to use technology to showcase themselves in ways that had previously been the domain of the small handful of superstars who qualified for Gatorade and McDonald's ads" (p.22). In Bosh's case, fans got to see another side of his personality not seen in press conferences, interviews or on the court.

Other athletes have taken heed of the potential of social media. Shaquielle O'Neal recently retired by linking a video on Tout to Twitter, making him the first player to announce his retirement directly to the fans instead of through journalism/news outlets. O'Neal has long been on the forefront of social media outreach, including like having ticket contests announced on his Twitter account. O'Neal's "Tag Shaq" ticket contest was a "friendly promotion" that "was a cool gesture to show he appreciates his fans and actually encourages them to approach him in public" (Rose, 2009). Through having social media at the control of his own fingertips, O'Neal took control of his right to publicity, much in the nature of Schilling, Bosh and others. It no longer took the team or traditional media to tell people who Shaq is. Shaq did so himself.

The athlete gaining some control over his or her publicity brings into question the role of publicists. For the most part, publicists play the role of organizer, as publicist Eddie Rhodman displayed in saying "my job is to get the word out about them—mostly via the media. That also includes planning events, scheduling appearances and creating strategic partnerships" (Mopwater, 2009). In this case, the media Rhodman is speaking of is not social media but news outlets. Nevertheless, with the rise of social media, publicity company Digital Royalty is taking heed of its power as they "develop digital integration and social media strategies for corporate and entertainment brands, professional athletes, sports teams and leagues" (Digital Royalty, 2011). Digital Royalty represents athletes like Shaquielle O'Neal, athlete/entertainment hybrids like Dwayne "The Rock" Johnson and the Ultimate Fighting Championship (UFC). Digital Royalty seems to encourage the relational aspect of social media, claiming "we're pioneers of zany ideas, like Shaquielle O'Neal's 'Random Acts of Shaqness', Hide and Tweets, Social Fan Phones and groundbreaking social media partnerships." Publicists seem to encourage athletes to get online and connect with fans, promoting the importance of having a relationship with those who support the sporting world.

O'Neal's actions had such an impact that they made Jalen Rose's list of the *5 Most Memorable Sports Tweets of 2009*, a specialty column on Mashable used to bring in the prospective of an athlete on other athletes using social media. Rose made his name as part of the famous "Fab Five" of the University of Michigan. The "Fab Five" were on the cutting edge of changes in basketball, including wearing baggie shorts, gloating, taunting, listening to hip hop and being the first team to have an all freshmen starting lineup. Thus, it can be seen that Rose has a unique perspective on changes in sports (and he is a social media user himself). Rose's list shows that what really makes the tweets of athletes interesting and worthwhile are those that give fans an access they have never had before. Included is O'Neal's Twitter contest, Lance Armstrong tweeting a picture of his newborn baby and New York Yankee pitcher Nick Swisher tweeting directly from the team's championship parade. Every one of these examples gave fans a level of access not provided in a stadium or through sports programming.

Leitch takes it to the next level by declaring that social media creates "a new way to experience sports" (2008, p. 15). Ben Parr, a writer for Mashable, illustrates this by discussing a feud that occurred between O'Neal and Dwight Howard, a center for the Orlando Magic, who at the time were vying for who was considered the NBA's best big man. The rivalry that grew between O'Neal and Howard transpired on Twitter so "it occurred in real-time for millions to see (Parr, 2008). Fans were able to see what was happening as it was happening. It "has given sports stars audiences of millions with whom they can directly communicate" (Parr, 2008). What this does is bring a "new, more personal aspect to sports that wasn't available just a few years ago" (Parr, 2008). All based on having a new level of access.

This feud between O'Neal and Howard brings to light a very important factor: that just because athletes have the ability to perform athletically does not mean they are exempt from natural human folly. Recently the Philadelphia Eagles' LeSean McCoy and the New York Giants' Osi Umenyiora have battled on Twitter, with McCoy basically calling Umenyiora soft and Umenyiora retorting that McCoy is a woman who does not deserve to be in the NFL. Prior to that, the Pittsburgh Steelers' Rashard Mendenhall tweeted about the death of Osama Bin Laden, saying that " 'We've only heard one side of the story'" and people needed to consider that a man had just died. Numerous people were offended by Mendenhall's seeming anti-Americanism, but "he said his words didn't come out the way he meant them" (Lopresti, 2011).

Nonetheless, his words were out there as stated. While fans do get to see into an athlete's life, that also means his or her flaws become readily apparent. With more access, more shall be known, which impacts the way the interaction goes and the relationship develops.

Schilling shows that in his blog. O'Neal shows that on his Twitter. Bosh did it in his videos. Numerous other athletes also choose to bring themselves onto social media and thus interact with fans. In such, it is changing the way fans relate to athletes. As Packard puts it:

> "Marketers have been trying to humanize athletes for years. When you can take athletes off their pedestals, you start to realize that beyond the money and tremendous athletic ability, many of them are not so different from us. For the first time, we have a direct outlet to almost all of them and they have a direct outlet to us.
>
> The athlete in the Twitter age has almost complete control over how the public views him or her and it will likely make or break many endorsement contracts in the near future. Big money is involved, and while many athletes will seize upon this as an opportunity to let their personality shine, others will rise and fall with their own mistakes" (2007).

Responding to this change, leagues have begun to create policies so as to not be improperly represented by athletes on social media. This does, in a sense, limit the connective capacity of fan and athlete by enforcing separate spheres to a degree. Major League Baseball does not allow any social media technology in the clubhouses 30 minutes before the game until the end of the game, while also prohibiting anything that can be conveyed as official MLB public communication, use of MLB entities on social media or divulging financial, medical or strategic information (Brown, 2011). The NFL and NBA both prohibit the use of social media during the games and for set periods of time before and after games (Stein 2009; Associated Press 2010). The PGA "is a firm believer in the power of social media to serve fans and expand the Tour's footprint around the world" and thus does not focus so much on policy as it does connection (Ramsey).

The PGA does have "over 40 players [who] can be found on Twitter." While they are not directly representing the Tour, golf being an individual, star driven sport means that the players indirectly represent the Tour more than any other athletes do their league. The basic etiquette of golf makes it easier for the PGA to not have a hard policy, like other leagues, because other players and the fans would consider it a violation of the game to use social media on course. Yet, being able to connect and build a relationship with players off the course can help it matter so much more what they do on the course.

However, none of these leagues' policies are as progressive as that of the UFC. Theirs is not so much a policy as it is a promotion. "The UFC's social media presence in sports is second only to the NBA's. UFC has more than 5.8 million combined Facebook fans and Twitter followers. That number does not factor in individual fighter's accounts, the company's Spanish-language social media accounts or (president Dana White's) massive reach" (Ortiz, 2011). Where UFC distinguished itself "at its recent UFC Fighter Summit, the company made headlines when it unveiled a $240,000 social media incentive program that will reward fighters for growing their presence on Twitter and putting out the most creative content" (2011). As Dana White put it " 'It's not only good for all of us (UFC), but when the fighters retire they have a built in fan-base" so "when they move on to that next chapter in their life and they continue to do other things, they're still connected with all these fans." The incentive program also combines with the fact that "UFC was the first professional sports league to broadcast live events on Facebook." In the end "the goal is to provide increased access to existing fans and to introduce the sport to a broader audience." White believes that this is done through creating a fan/athlete connection resulting in a lasting relationship where a fan cares about an athlete and athlete cares about a fan. Parasocial relationships turned up a notch.

LITERATURE REVIEW: SOCIALOGICAL ASPECTS OF ANALYSIS

The sociological aspect of this change is important in order to give ground to the ideas by which analysis will find definition. Judith Butler's ideas on performivity are the first factor of this. As Butler sees it, everyone in society is playing roles, which are created by the historical roles understood through the past. She focuses on gender, but the fan and athlete also have historical roles, so it is plausible to apply her ideas there as well. The main way that these roles come to be defined is through what Butler calls "linguistic constructions," or the way we communicate with one another (Felluga). Erving Goffman says that because we use certain ways to communicate with each other "we are 'sign vehicles': our body idiom conveys information about ourselves and our social relationships" (p. 8). The way that we decide to communicate, be it social media, text message, phone call, in person, etc., says something about our communication, our self and the relationships we maintain. Goffman declared us "sign vehicles" because we carry these aspects about our selves into the way we communicate. Both Butler and Goffman brought their ideas about before social media, and now that a major portion of communication is happening there, their ideas may be adapted to the new communicative outlet. These communicative interactions build how we come to understand our realities.

In coming to understand this reality, we create what Goffman called a "frame." We use these to "identify what is taking place," like in understanding a joke from a lesson or a friend from a family member. When regarding the fan/athlete interaction, this frame is being rebuilt because a new element was brought in: social media. Since Butler sees reality as constructed by how we interact, when that interaction shifts or has a new element brought in, change comes. Therefore, the frame within which the reality has been constructed is also altered. The new frame also redefines the rules of interaction, which can be changed because "those rules are historical and rely on their continual citation or enactment by subject, then they can be challenged and changed through alternative performative acts" (Felluga). Change the rules, change the reality.

Within this new frame there are limits that need be understood. As Daniel Solove claims, an individual is not seen in totality in one forum (Solove, 2007). Thus, neither fan nor athlete can be fully understood from an online interaction. It is a piece of the whole, which ties back to Butler seeing that there are multiple roles of performivity where there are distinctions of self that support different aspects of the established status quo. People play out different roles in different places to fit within the frame, such as in political, private, communal, religious, etc. Understood this way, a fan will never fully comprehend an athlete's whole person solely through social media, even though it does bring them in closer to the athlete.

This is an aspect of the right of the athlete to control publicity, in that he or she gets to keep private certain points of his or her life.

Social media has recreated the fan/athlete interaction, thus creating a new style relationship between the two. What comes about are fresh roles, a different frame and a changing dynamic of the public and privates selves of athletes.

METHOD

It is important that a sports fan, such as myself, be the one to construct this paper because as a sports fan I have relationship with athletes. An outsider may not be able to fully comprehend such a relationship because he or she has not been a part of, nor experienced the emotion of it.

Still the same, just being a sports fan is not enough to have a complete understanding of this new dynamic, at least in the academic sense. Thus, I have taken some important steps in my method of approach.

First, I explored academic articles about the relationship between fans and athletes, both when dealing with the Internet and when not. If this was not done, and I was defining the new relationship purely on my own experience, there would be the potential that I am an anomaly and thus bring nothing worthwhile to the whole. Exploring such papers allows me to understand how other fans consume sports and put myself within the spectrum of things, therefore allowing me to use myself as a relative basis for analysis. It should be noted that I am not an anomaly, according to my reading of the literature.

Additionally, I paired articles written by sports journalists with the aforementioned articles, in order to gain a deeper understanding of the opinion about sports and social media's union. The journalists are fans as well, thus the relational aspect comes into play. Looking at the work of sports journalists brings in the views of other fans for me to analyze and compare my perspective to.

Lastly, I employed participant observation by using myself, the researcher, as a research instrument. To do so I took one week (June 16-23), which had special events, such as the U.S. Open and NBA Draft, in it and part of the week with normal sporting events. I intensely journaled about my experience through the week, looking at how I acted on social media sites when dealing with athletes and sports. By doing so I was able to have an in depth look at the fan experience. When journaling, I particularly focused on things I deemed to be phenomena. I defined phenomena as something that stood out from the plethora of happenings on social media sites. Analyzing these phenomena allowed for me to gain an understanding of what is happening in the whole.

ANALYSIS

Social media has created a whole new way that people move through life in the world of sports. The effect of this is a new relationship between fans and athletes that is changing sports. Prior to social media there was the barrier, but social media battles against that by promoting interaction. Blogs are an online journal where people can directly see one's thoughts, even an athlete's. Facebook is based on people connecting with others, such as friends, family, peers and others in the world who matter to them in some form. Twitter is all about being able to see the thoughts of someone on the happenings of the world and how they go through their day-to-day life.

For fan and athlete, the ability to connect like this can be seen in many ways. Schilling's blog, O'Neal's contests and Bosh's YouTube videos are major examples of this. Personally, I experienced this connective capability during my week of journaling; such as tweeting about Rory McIlroy after his U.S. Open win on June 19, saying "Congrats Rory!!! A class act, hard worker and very deserving," or in following the Green Bay Packer's championship ring ceremony on June 16, even tweeting directly to receiver Greg Jennings, saying "@GregJennings need to see pics man!! Go @pack." Before social media, being able to communicate directly with athletes did not happen on an everyday basis.

Certainly there are the limits of league rules and athletes having to worry about the publicity factor. Yet, for the most part it does not seem that these inhibit the connection between the two groups. For example, Digital Royalty actually encourages its clients to interact with fans, as does UFC. For professional sports leagues, athletes are really only limited from using social media during games, media time and in some cases team time. Moreover, they are not allowed to post about official business of team or league.

But as a fan, I cannot see anything during these times that really restrains my being able to see the athlete as a fellow human. During the games, I want to see the athlete perform, not tweet. Further, I would not enjoy seeing athletes tweet the news, because they could have misinformation. I would rather see their thoughts and feelings on the news. One example of this is when Spurs guard Danny Green tweeted about the Spurs trading teammate George Hill on draft night, June 23, saying he was going to miss his "bro." Another is being able to see what McIlroy did after his tournament win, where he tweeted a view from the press conference table and celebrating with the trophy on June 19. As a fan, I have a grasp on the reality that like any person athletes have obligations. This also circles back to the idea that the full self cannot be seen in one forum. There are pieces of an athlete's life that fans simply are limited in accessing or cannot access at all.

However, with social media fans are still getting to see more of the athlete as person as opposed to the athlete as competitor or performer. I noted in my journal that I related to McIlroy because I saw bits of myself in him, namely that he was tweeting pictures of himself with the U.S. Open trophy after his victory. I reacted to this by stating "he is only one year older than I am and so seeing that he does the same things I believe I would do if I won my favorite major really builds a connection." I also noticed that the tweeting of pictures by the Green Bay Packers at their ring ceremony and the contest held by Green Bay Packer Tom Crabtree "makes athletes seem normal to fans. If it were me and I have a Super Bowl championship ring and the opportunity to share in my championship with fans, I certainly would." Other athletes, like Jermichael Finley, Chad Ochocinco and Colt McCoy tweet about the daily happenings of their lives, allowing fans to see that "athletes go through the same day to day kind of things that we 'everyday' folks go through." Now fans get to see what athletes are thinking, feeling, doing, what excites them, what their passions are, etc.

Another dimension of fans gaining an understanding of the person an athlete is comes through seeing athletes interact with one another online. When the Green Bay Packers were having their championship ring ceremony, numerous players were tweeting about the experience so the fans could see how athletes went through the same experience. George Hill and San Antonio Spur Dejaun Blair, who are known for being great friends, interact with one another on Twitter for fans to see. When Hill was traded on June 23, Green's tweet about how "he was upset that his 'bro' George Hill was leaving" gave an eye into their connection. These are things beyond the "we played as hard as we could" chatter of media interviews or staged publicity presentations that happen at organized events. It is more raw and realistic. Fans are getting the opportunity to see something that used to be completely cut off from them, even if the fans are only on the fringes.

But the increased access to athletes is not all a superfluous joy and sunshine. Take the past feud between Shaquielle O'Neal and Dwight Howard, which is one of the first notable feuds to play out online, as an example. In the past, athletes "would say something and ESPN or the local sports section would run with it" but now "Twitter's mainstream adoption has given sports stars audiences of millions with whom they can directly communicate" leading to " a new, more personal aspect to sports that wasn't available just a few years ago" (Parr, 2008). By O'Neal and Howard playing out their rivalry online fans got to see directly what the athletes thought of one another and thus see a different side of both players. With less distance between fan and athlete the flaws and points of admiration shine equally. Take Reshard Mendenhall and his infamous tweet about the death of Osama Bin Laden. Lopresti points out "just because a guy can score touchdowns—or act in movies—doesn't mean he's any wiser about world events than your postal carrier" (2011). Other slip-ups by sports figures such as Antonio Cromartie, Ozzie Guillen and Larry Johnson are further examples of this.

On June 20, while I was journaling, I watched a NFL Network video about the Twitter battle that went on between LeSean McCoy of the Philadelphia Eagles and the New York Giant's Osi Umenyiora, with the two engaging in name calling and disputes over each other's manhood (NFL Enterprises, 2011). It got quite heated and I pointed out that "it is a total change because the battles between players are going on directly in front of the fans" as fans are able to see the battles, disputes and rivalries between players before journalists have the opportunity to report them. For instance, the video that I watched was one reacting to, as opposed to reporting, the actions of McCoy and Umenyiora. No person is without flaw, yet there is a tendency within fans to build up athletes because they get the opportunity to do what only a small percentage of people get to do, not only in playing their games but also in having the wealth and experiences allotted to athletes in today's day and age.

Jimmy Sanderson shows one possible reason for this happening in his analysis of Curt Schilling's blog. Sanderson says, "professional athletes are quite insulated from the general public, and are often privileged throughout the course of their athletic careers" (2010, p.201). Therefore, athletes have a different sense of "reality" because the social construction of their lives is somewhat different from the everyman. Fans, like myself, who put athletes on a pedestal and live vicariously through them, create this social construction. As a result, as much as it is pleasant to see that athletes are just like "you and me" it can be hard to see that they are flawed like "you and me."

Still the same, seeing the flaws of an athlete does not seem to inhibit a fan's desire to interact with the athlete. Rather, as my experience shows, it makes the athlete seem more human, thus creating a sense that athletes do not live in some far off fairy tale. In my journal there is a telling note that "I tweet much in the same fashion as athletes" by tweeting about my workouts, other day-to-day happenings of my life, using their catchphrases or providing inspiration. For example, some of my tweets include "it's Friday, let's take greatness by the throat and show it how we roll"(June 16); "good workout, good meeting, good smoothie. Guess I should go to work and make that money now"(June 20); "husband and wife come to the store in the EXACT same clothes. Shoes and all! #HOP[Hold On Player] #comeonman" (using Deion Sander's catchphrases) (June 21); and "half the family up for early morning workouts. Beast mode this…" (June 25). Furthermore, I tweeted about my thoughts on the happenings of the sports world, which athletes also do. Some examples of those tweets are "congratulations to all my @packers for getting your rings today"(June

16); "I think Chris Singleton from FSU will be the sleeper of the #NBADraft"(June 23); and "CORY FRIGGIN' JOSEPH!!! Kid can play defense, pass and has a ton of room to grow"(June 23). I deem this "has something to do with my desire to be a professional athlete, like I am imitating them so as to live vicariously through them." In other words, I put them on a pedestal as something greater than myself, something I desire to be. Having social media for us to interact means I have an even greater capability to know what it is that I am vicariously living through, in both the good and the bad.

The human factor of seeing an athlete's good and bad qualities encourages interaction through making them seem more like an everyman, making the relationship ever stronger. For the fan, particularly an avid one like myself, this raises the level of emotionally connection with the athlete and justifies support, much like one would support his or her friends despite their not being perfect. Take my following of Michael Vick, quarterback for the Philadelphia Eagles who is famous and infamous for the dog-fighting ring he ran that led him to serve a prison term. Certainly Vick is far from perfect and it would be easy to condemn him, yet I follow him on Twitter because he has presented himself, in public and online, as one who is genuinely regretful for the mistakes of his past. Admittedly I began following Vick to see if the way he was appearing on ESPN was really who he was, but after following him for a period of time I made the decision to remain a follower because he seems like a redemption story with which I can connect. No one is perfect, fan or athlete, and knowing so brings the two groups closer together.

No longer is the athlete completely insulated, nor is the fan barred from the happenings of the sports community. Now the fan lives on the fringes, but still gets to see in, which is a new reality. I journaled numerous examples of the reality of the relationship, such as when Rory McIlroy won the U.S. Open on June 19 "within an hour of his win, 'Congrats Rory' was trending on Twitter." The next day, Tom Crabtree of the Green Bay Packers held a contest on his Twitter, to which I responded, "I thought it was really interesting to see how Crabtree was interacting with his fans. He did not have to do it, but did so that he could interact with his fans." My direct tweets to Greg Jennings, Tom Crabtree and Luke Donald further bear that interaction creates a new type of closeness, breaking the barrier and building relationships. In all cases, the fan or the athlete made the effort to engage with the other. Through making this choice, both support the relationship being cultivated.

Which brings to the forefront the thought of what this means for the relationship of fans and athletes. Sanderson points out "support was generated from blog readers, who mobilized as a collective support group for Schilling" because they appreciated him as a player and the fact that he is a human being and has an opinion (p. 201). Thus, the connection between fan and athlete becomes more about interaction, in turn being more relational.

A base of this new relationship is found in that being able to interact means athletes and fans now work in a horizontal support system. In the past the interaction was more vertical, where fans consumed the sports and supported the athletes by doing so. The most support that athletes gave fans was in competing, but it is arguable that this was more athlete-focused as well. This reality is being broken in favor of one wherein fan and athlete can now lift each other up directly. Take the examples of my tweeting congratulations to the Packers and Rory McIlroy, or tweeting to George Hill after he was traded by saying "@George_Hill3 you will be missed. best of luck in your home state (don't beat up on us too much)" (June 23).

Part of this horizontal support comes in the form of retweets. In my journal I recorded that "fans are constantly asking athletes for retweets. It is like a badge of honor. A souvenir or some sort. Today (June 22) I saw a guy ask for one of the Packers to retweet his tweet in honor of his girlfriend's birthday." Personally I have not asked any athletes for a retweet, but "I think it is a really cool thing for athletes to do because they can show fans individually that they matter." It is a transaction that is vastly different from an autograph or souvenir from the stadium because it is on more of an individual basis. It also continues the support system because fans are requesting the athlete's retweet because he or she is someone from whom a retweet is valuable. The athlete actually retweeting shows support for the fan being a fan. Athletes comply with such requests, which results in another break in the wall of the parasocial. The screen is still there, but it is now a piece of the relationship instead of a barrier. The screen is becoming a tool for the interaction.

The next aspect of this relationship comes by athletes bringing fans closer to the sporting world, showing them things that fans previously had never been able to see. Fans can now sit with Rory McIlroy at his U.S. Open press conference or be with the Green Bay Packers during their ring ceremony. Nick Swisher tweeting from the Yankees championship parade and Lance Armstrong tweeting the first pictures of his baby are other examples. But in my own experience with during the Packer's ring ceremony, "I actually sat waiting for new tweets to appear. Didn't get a lot done tonight, needless to say. Still, it felt worth it (and not just because the ring is awesome!) because I felt like I was part of something. This is probably as close as I will ever get to a ring ceremony, despite them being in Wisconsin while I sit in Texas. I felt like I was there" (June 16). Fans used to be totally outside as an observer. When the Packer's won their last championship (1996), I never would have been able to participate in the ceremony in such a sense. This can further be seen by the tweets of Hope Solo, the goalie for the USA soccer team that lost in the finals of the 2011 World Cup. Much like fans could not see into the 1996 Packers championship run, fans could not see into the 1999 Women's World Cup run when Team USA won the championship. This time around though, Solo was able to take fans through the excitement leading up to the match with Japan, the agony of defeat, overcoming that defeat and the media tour she went on after returning from Germany. Now, fans are brought into aspects of sporting culture they did not have access to before, albeit on the fringes. This happens when what used to limit interaction, a screen, becomes the centerpiece of interaction. The barrier is further busted.

A relationship now existing between fan and athlete means that the roles between the two are being redefined, ever shaped by the changes that online interaction brings. As Butler claims "rules are historical and rely on their continual citation or enactment by subjects" (Felluga). No longer are fan or athlete participating in this historical definition of what their roles should be. Now fan and athlete are redefining those roles.

For the fan, the focus of this is found in following the athlete and providing support directly to the person. It may even go as far as mimicking them. Fans doing so encourages the athlete to continue to have an online presence because he or she sees that doing so matters to the fans. Bosh realized that he had the ability to reach people previously beyond him and show them that he enjoyed goofing off with friends like most people do. O'Neal was able to manipulate social media to connect with the fans in his "Tag Shaq" ticket contests. On his blog, Schilling had support "generated from blog readers, who mobilized as a collective support group" (Sanderson, 2010, p. 201).

For athletes this new role is part supporter, through things like the ticket contests or retweets. But for the most part, the athlete serves in his or her new role as a reporter of sorts. The athlete now reports what he or she is doing, gaining control over his or her publicity and moving beyond the traditional publicity received in news outlets. In my journal there are the ever present examples of the multiple Packers players tweeting from the ring ceremony, where I said "I felt like I was a part of something," Nick Collins tweeting about the enjoyment he receives from holding youth football camps, where I noted "it was cool to be able to see what athletes actually think about doing camps like that" (June 20) and Clay Matthews tweeting from a photo shoot, where I wrote that "it's nice to be able to see a glimpse into what players do off the field" (June 21), Solo was also able to do this by taking fans through the media tour she went on post-World Cup, even posting pictures of herself at *Good Morning America* and other places across Hollywood. Fans come to know players based on how they present themselves, or what Goffman called their "identity pegs." These identity pegs are attributes about an individual that help show whom he or she is as a person. The athletes are now able to define who they want to be and what their identity pegs are because they are presenting themselves to the fan in a direct manner. No longer is the athlete subject to the media's presentation of them.

The relational aspect of social media interaction brings about a community. This community evolves as the "frame" presented in Goffman's theories, which he claims helps individuals gain an understanding of their reality. This frame is a new type of parasocial relationship, because there is still a physical barrier between the fan and the athlete. In spite of that, this hurdle is being reshaped because fans and athletes are now using technology to connect and are building a sporting community of relationship. In turn the framework that fans and athletes are working in is broader.

An interesting aspect of this community goes back to the fact that fans now have an eye into the humanity of athletes for they see the positive and negative aspects of the individual as he or she presents herself online. Plausibly, when fans see athletes rivaling online the fan could join in the debate. However, as a part of this community I have never felt obliged to tweet against an athlete. I see the rivalries as part of the spectacle of sports and therefore a piece of this social media based community, thus I observe it but do not partake. It is not a piece of my role. Nonetheless, there are points when fans do get up in arms, such as when Mendenhall tweeted about Bin Laden. The fact that it was reported in the news, with his recant of his statement due to the fans uproar a piece of the article by Lopresti, shows that this community does hold athletes accountable the same as an everyday person. Violations of norms, be they political, social, religious, etc., are no more accepted online than in the physical world, nor are they accepted by athlete or fan.

In the end, while this is enjoyable for the fan and may even support his or her sense of self (which it certainly did for me as I was able to see my support of athletes and enjoyment of watching them was worthwhile through their posts), it redefines how athletes are able to move through the world. They do not have to succumb to how others present them. Rather, they create how the world perceives them. Chris Bosh is able to let fans know he is a little goofy; Jermichael Finley gets to take fans through his rehab instead of depending on the media to provide updates; Clay Matthews gets to show what a photo shoot is like as opposed having fans wait until the advertisement or magazine comes out; Rory McIlroy gets to thank fans directly for their support; Hope Solo is able to show herself preparing for media interviews and share her emotions after a crushing loss. Now athletes get to present themselves in a manner desirable to them instead of having to work in order to have the news report about them in a sense they deem appropriate.

It is important to note what the athletes do not tweet, put on Facebook, etc. Looking at this is essential since once an athlete puts something on social networking sites it becomes very much a public piece of information. Thus, what is not put on there are things the athletes plausibly prefer to keep private. This can also be deemed part of the self that the athletes do not wish to present in this setting, therefore supporting Butler and Solove's comprehension of a person as a sum of parts created through different parts of society. While Jermichael Finley tweets about his family, he has not tweeted on dates with his wife. George Hill tweeted thanks to San Antonio Spurs fans for their support, although he did not tweet about if he had any meetings with team officials or foresight into the trade. Players tend not to tweet or post about what they think teams should do, emotional situations, relationship statuses or the serious happenings of their homes. Since athletes feed what gets out, they can also filter what gets out and thus affect the way that society perceives them. Being in a position of publicity, this is one of the new functions social media allows them, and is essential to how individual athletes choose to cultivate relationships with their fans, as they determine the level of engagement and connection they will partake in.

It could be argued that news outlets would report what athletes do not present online. However, through my time-consuming sports news, I have noticed that this is not the case. Rather, news outlets have taken what athletes put online and reported on that, such as the McCoy/Umenyiora dispute or Solo's tweets building up to the World Cup final. It appears that news outlets find enough to report through these online forums and traditional means, thus they respect the pieces of an athlete's life he or she does not present online.

Athletes now, like never before, are the masters of their right to publicity and controllers of the way they are perceived. By being able to do so, and not depending on media to create it, athletes are able to engage fans and build a relationship because they control the level of engagement.

CONCLUSION

The purpose of this paper has been to display how the shifting norms in sports and how fans and athletes being able to come directly to one another have altered the sports landscape. I have laid a groundwork for understanding the changes that are still going on by showing that interaction between the two previously separate groups has made a relationship and brought two spheres into one community, where interaction and relations are key.

This is only the beginning. I have created an outline for understanding, but even as these words are read the Internet is ever changing. That is its nature, what defines it. Thus, as new pieces of the Internet come about, such as Google+, Tout, Klout, etc., it is essential for an analysis to be done about how these new technologies alter and develop the relationship, plus what it means for sports. In the grand scheme of things, we now know the game that is being played. Nevertheless, the first quarter is just underway.

References

About dR. (2011). Retrieved 2011, from http://www.thedigitalroyalty.com/about/

Brown, W. J., Basil, M. D., & Bocarnea, M. C. (2003). The Influence of Famous Athletes on Health Beliefs and Practices: Mark McGwire, Child Abuse Prevention, and Androstenedione. *Journal of Health Communication, 8*, 41-57. Retrieved from Academic Search Complete database.

Deveney, S. (2010, March 1). A SELF-MADE STAR. *The Sporting News*, 20-23.

Felluga, D. (2011). *Modules on Butler: On Performativity*. Retrieved from http://www.cla.purdue.edu/english/theory/genderandsex/modules/butlerperformativity.html

Gregory, S. (2009, May 18). The Tweet Hereafter. *Sports Illustrated, 110*(20), 14-15.

Grove, J. V. (2009, September 5). Sports and Social Media: Where Opportunity and Fear Collide. *Mashable*. Retrieved from http://mashable.com/2009/09/05/sports-and-social-media/

League announces policy on social media for before and after games . (2010). *Associated Press*. Retrieved from http://www.nfl.com/news/story?id=09000d5d8124976d&template=without-video-with-comments&confirm=true

Leitch, W. (2009). How tweet it is. *The Sporting News*, 15.

Lopresti, M. (2011, May 5). Tapped-out: Abusing anti-social media. *USA Today*. Retrieved from Academic Search Complete database.

Major League Baseball Social Media Policy. (2011, May 1). *The Biz of Baseball*. Retrieved from http://www.bizofbaseball.com/index.php?option=com_content&view=article&id=5191:older-undated-version-of-mlb-social-media-policy&catid=7:selection-of-docs&Itemid=25

Mullman, J. (2010, July 26). Want to Score in Sports? Create a Connection CAA Sports' Michael Levine on the Impact of Social Media, Scandals and NBA Free Agency. *Advertising Age*. Retrieved from http://adage.com/article/special-report-sports-marketing-2010/sports-marketing-q-a-caa-sports-michael-levine/145074/

The NBA's Social Media Policy. (2009, October 1). *SLAM Online*. Retrieved from http://www.slamonline.com/online/nba/2009/10/the-nbas-social-media-policy/

Ortiz, M. B. (2011, June 6). Dana White leads UFC into social realm. *ESPN.com*. Retrieved from http://sports.espn.go.com/espn/page2/story?page=burnsortiz/110606_ufc_dana_white

Packard, W. (2010, June). How Digital Media Is Changing the Sports Experience. *Mashable*. Retrieved from http://mashable.com/2011/06/17/digital-media-sports/

Parr, B. (2009, June 6). Shaq vs. Dwight Howard on Twitter, and What It Means for Sports. *Mashable*. Retrieved from http://mashable.com/2009/06/06/shaq-twitter-dwight-howard/

Ramsey, C. (n.d.). How the PGA Tour Uses Social Media to Connect with Fans. *More Than Creative*. Retrieved from http://www.morethancreative.com/2010/02/how-the-pga-tour-uses-social-media-to-connect-with-fans/

Rose, J. (2009, December 11). 5 Most Memorable Sports Tweets of 2009 [Web log post]. Retrieved from http://mashable.com/2009/12/11/sports-tweets/

Sanderson, J. (2010, April). "The Nation Stands Behind You": Mobilizing Social Support on 38pitches.com. *Communication Quarterly, 58*(2), 188–206.

Schroeder, S. (2011, June). 2012 Olympic Athletes Are Welcome To Tweet. *Mashable*. Retrieved from http://mashable.com/2011/06/27/olympic-2012-games-tweet/

Shain, J. (2011, February 16). PGA Tour does full U-turn on mobile devices Once banned, cell phones now outlet for social media. *Orlando Sentinel*. Retrieved from http://articles.orlandosentinel.com/2011-02-16/sports/os-pro-golf-insider-column-0217-20110216_1_cell-phones-mobile-devices-social-media

Solove, D. J. (2007). *the future of reputation*. New Haven and London: Yale University Press.

Stein, M. (2009, September 30). NBA social media guidelines out. *ESPN.com*. Retrieved from http://sports.espn.go.com/nba/news/story?id=4520907

Sun, T. (2010, June). Antecedents and Consequences of Parasocial Interaction with Sport Athletes and Identification with Sport Teams. *Journal of Sport Behavior, 33*(2), 194-217. Retrieved from Academic Search Complete database.

Test Drive My Job:: Atlanta-Based Sports Publicist Eddie Rhodman, Jr. (2009, September 15). *Mopwater PR*. Retrieved from http://www.millerlittlejohnmedia.com/2009/09/15/test-drive-my-job-atlanta-based-sports-publicist-eddie-rhodman-jr/

Twitter. (2011). Retrieved 2011, from Twitter website: http://twitter.com

Twitter war of words [Video file]. (2011, June 20). Retrieved from http://prod.www.nfl.com/videos/nfl-

network-total-access/09000d5d82067ad8/Twitter-war-of-words

7 Faking Freedom in a World of Conformity: How Military LipDub Serves Capitalism: A Critical Ethnography of the Military "Lip Dub": A Case Study on the HMM-266 Marines YouTube Video

By
Aubry L. Buzek

In the military lip dub video I analyze, I found that the social hierarchies of these deployed Marines everyday lives are overturned, and their suppressed desires are realized through this video, a Carnival in the digital world. The ambivalence of the laughter in the video is shown in the austere landscape of Camp Leatherneck as it turns into a stage for performing, unknown junior-enlisted Marines becoming well-known pop stars, war stresses becoming joy, and stifled feelings finding a voice for expression.

Although the Marines are expressing their suppressed desires through the military lip dub form as Carnivalesque in a celebration of liberation, this form in fact has detrimental effects to the free will of those in it because it provides even more power to those who it is supposed to oppose. Capitalism allows the media and military to gain control and power from this form, and contrary to their intentions the people become even more subject and trapped by its rituals and laws.

Literature Review

The history and breadth of study of the rhetorical artifact I am investigating is, from what I know, very limited if not non-existent. The video has existed for about three months, so from what I can tell I am the first to study this artifact.

The genre has some limited study. This military lip dub is a small category that exists in the larger genre of the Internet meme, which has been researched by mostly amateur bloggers and tech writers. According to the New Media Research Studio, "the Internet meme has no particular purpose or meaning inherent of the person creating it" ("The Internet Meme: A Joyous Thing of Laughter," 2011).

The next argument is helpful in that it helps solidify my argument that a viral video doesn't need a utilitarian motive to be successful, but the success of it may have a utilitarian effect by shaping the society that views it.

Jean Burgess argues in "All your Chocolate Rain are Belong to Us? Viral Video, Youtube and the Dynamics of Participatory Culture," that "viewed from the perspective of cultural participation rather than marketing, videos are not messages, and neither are they products that are distributed via social networks. Rather, they are the mediating mechanisms via which cultural practices are originated, adopted and (sometimes) retained within social networks."

Burgess continues his argument by saying that these Internet memes or viral videos are "mediators of ideas that are taken up in practice within social networks." These ideas spread because new masses and individuals transform them. One of the more important arguments gleaned from Burgess' paper is that these meme viral videos "are spoiled by going mainstream…and have relatively short shelf lives."

This is important to note because although the evolution and popularity of these military lip dub videos or lip dub videos in general may be in their height, at some point viewers will lose interest. I believe the long-term effects the videos have on society, however, may be more viral than the videos themselves. The video could possibly create a better equipped vehicle for delivering social views to the masses, and whether or not the Internet meme military lip dub lives or dies the residual effects will stay.

Clay Shirky argues in his book "Cognitive Surplus" that certain creative acts on the Internet serve no civic purpose and their only real purpose is to garner humor, like "Lolcats," one popular Internet meme. Lolcats emerged from the web site "I can Haz Cheezburger?" where users take a picture of a cat and put a quirky expression over it as if a cat would be speaking. He says that they are "formed quickly and with a minimum of craft...the social value of a whoopee cushion and the cultural life span of a mayfly." Although that may be, he says their value is the message they send "You can play this game too" (Shirky, 2010).

This idea about the value of Internet memes being in their ability to create communities and a sense of sharing is very important to analyzing the military lip dub, because it is a very similar meme to Lolcats. Although it may have more social and political relevance than a Lolcat, the motivation behind creating the lip dub is the awareness of those that came before it, trying to improve upon them and share them with the people. This wasn't some organic creation, the military lip dub and lip dubs in general follow "internally consistent rules," which the Marines follow in this video.

Although the artifact and the study of its genre have limited study, the medium of the artifact has quite a bit of scholarly interest.

Jean Burgess and Joshua Green write in "Youtube: Online Video and Participatory Culture," that "its important not to fall into the trap of simply assuming that vernacular video is organized primarily around a desire to broadcast the self. Viewed as a form of 'vernacular creativity,' the creation and sharing of videos functions culturally as a means of social networking as opposed to a mode of cultural production" (Burgess, 2009).

This is important in my analysis of the video because it explains how the motive of creating a video is the sharing and the need to create a community and dialogue.

In "Publicly Private and Privately Public: Social Networking on Youtube" Patricia Lange shows that "the public and private fractalize in complex ways in video making and sharing on YouTube...watching media is not merely a passive exercise, but rather that film or video viewing in general involves active interpretations that shape reception of media messages. On YouTube, frequent interaction between video makers

and viewers is a core component of participation on the site" (Lange, 2007).

This is important because it shows that the success of a video on Youtube isn't its entertainment value as it would be on television, but the entertainment, interpretation and community that are all encompassed on the Youtube page.

In order to better analyze this artifact, I will be utilizing Mikhail Bakhtins theory of Carnivalesque. Bakhtin argues that "Carnival is the place for working out a new mode of interrelationship between individuals . . . People who in life are separated by impenetrable hierarchical barriers enter into free and familiar contact on the Carnival square" (Bakhtin, p. 123). There is a motivation during Carnival time to create a form of human social configuration that 'lies beyond existing social forms'" (Lechte, 2007).

Bakhtin expands upon this idea of Carnivalesque providing a venue for social change by providing several stipulations about what Carnival is and isn't. Carnival isn't officially sanctioned or a holiday, it isn't quantitative or causal logic of science and seriousness, and it never reinforces the prevailing regime of everyday life. In Carnival, the people are the actors/spectators and subjects/objects of laughter, while the officialdom, whether it be the government or even religion, is subject to its rituals and laws. "To put it in a nutshell: Carnival is not simply negative; it has no utilitarian motive. It is…ambivalent." (Lechte, 2007).

The importance of Carnivalesque lies in laughter, but this laughter has no object, is not purely parodic, ironical or satirical and is not equated with any specific forms, it is ambivalent. Bakhtin describes Carnival laughter as one of the "essential forms of truth concerning the world," and that it embraces lowness, particularly that of degradation, debasement and the body and all of its functions. (Lechte, 2007).

The theory of Carnival also highlights the ambivalence of Carnival figures, such as clowns or the actors/participants in masks. These characters reveal the ambivalence and all-embracing logic of Carnival. The mask itself is always obviously distorting in Carnival, and reveals and plays with contradictions. The mask also signifies the loss of individuality and the assumption of anonymity, which creates an assumption of multiple identities. Bakhtin writes that the mask is "connected with the joy of change and reincarnation, with gay relativity and with the merry negation of uniformity and similarity." (Lechte, 2007).

Method

The analysis or popular culture criticism that follows is based on a critical ethnographic case study of the video and user comments on it over a one month period from May 2011 to June 2011. The data includes field notes on observations of the video and analysis of 500 user comments.

The beginning of my research began with the question, "how do service members use Youtube?" which I thought was an interesting aspect of living privately in public, (the theme of this volume).

I began by using five different search terms to compile and aggregate all of the different types of videos that popped up when the preferences were set to "in exact search results order" and "filtered by view count." The search terms used were "U.S. Military," "U.S. Marine Corps," "U.S. Air Force," "U.S. Army" and "U.S. Navy." I added every relevant (military related) video to a word processing file, where I added the web link, title of the video and view count.

From there, I watched the videos and started to code them into certain categories. I coded until I started running out of new categories, and ended up with 12 different categories. At one point every video I found could be sorted into one of these. The categories included: Photo Slideshow/Video Montage, Music Video/Dance, Military Humor, Military Bloopers/Accidents, Military Tribute, Combat Operations, Weapons/Capabilities, Drill Team/Guard/Ceremony, Reunions, Boot Camp/Training and

UFO's.

After sorting the videos into these categories, interesting patterns based on view counts began to emerge. I found that of all of categories of military videos on Youtube, the ones with the most consistently high view counts fell into the category of "Music Video/Dance," which I eventually figured out were lip dubs. I found this pattern interesting, considering what I thought was the lack of social/political relevance compared to combat operations or even recruiting.

I decided I wanted to explore this phenomenon further, and rather than try and aggregate information about every popular military lip dub on Youtube I decided to do a critical ethnographic case study of one, so I could get as much detail and spend as much effort researching within my time constraints as possible.

Around the time of my beginning research, the Marines from HMM-266 doing the Britney Spears song was very popular and covered on the news. It had been on Youtube for a relatively short time, and had almost 3 million views, which is pretty high compared to the view counts of other military related Youtube videos such as recruiting, bloopers and weapons systems. Also, it was talked about on news shows and entertainment shows when Britney Spears publicly announced her support for it and extended an invitation to the Marines to attend one of her concerts. I decided that this particular video was a great example of the military lip dub and would be perfect for my research and analysis.

In order to analyze the video, the ethnographic process provided me with the data needed to apply the theory of Carnivalesque, which is a form of early structuralism.

The early structuralism movement was set in motion by the focus on "society as a system where certain phenomena constitute a 'total social fact,'" shifting toward an explanation on society based on its content and toward a "focus on form as structural (that is differential and relational)….history constructs the intellectual framework that comprehends it" (Lechte, 2007).

The intellectual framework behind my explaining and analyzing this video is my own understanding of technology, society and the military in the present, which is important in being true to early structuralism ideas. I will use Bakhtin's theory of Carnivalesque in order to apply my own intellectual framework to explain my views of the social relevance of the form of the military lip dub, taking this particular video as an example

Although Bakhtin formally distanced himself from structuralism, according to Lechte "his refusal to embrace the ideology of the author's intentions as a way of explaining the meaning of a work of art, places him much closer to a structural approach than might at first appear." "Bakhtin rejects what he sees as the structuralist tendency to analyze texts as though they were completely self-contained units whose meaning could be established independently of context. Rather, any attempt to understand parole [speech] must take into account the circumstances, assumptions and the time of the enunciation of the utterance. In effect, Bakhtin urges that account must be taken of the contingency of language" (Lechte, 2007).

This is important for me to understand in order to effectively analyze the video using Bakhtins theory of Carnivalesque. What I get from early structuralism and Bakhtin's embrace/rebuttal of it is that I need to try to explain the relevance of the form of the military lipdub using my own intellectual framework in the present, and all the circumstances, assumptions, and time factors that go along with it, while realizing that it's not my intentions that are the explanation of the video.

Analysis

The video I'm analyzing of the the deployed U.S. Marines from Marine Heavy Helicopter Squadron 266 (Reinforced) Britney Spears "Hold It Against Me" lip dub video had received more than 3.5 million views by July 2011, about 3 months after it was originally posted. The video featured 19 mostly junior enlisted Marines from the squadron lip-synching and dancing to the Britney Spears song "Hold it Against Me" amidst the backdrop of the flight line at Camp Leatherneck in Afghanistan. The video shows the deployed Marines performing on the flight line and at the squadron's hangar in mostly utility uniforms and flight suits.

The popular song draws attention to the young, mostly male masculine Marines performing at odds to

Britney Spears voice, lyrics and dance moves. The lyrics themselves deal mainly with themes of sexual

tension. The main appeal of the song is the dance beat and production value.

Hey over there
Please forgive me
If I'm coming on too strong
Hate to stare
But you're winning
And they're playing my favorite song

So come here
A little closer
Wanna whisper in your ear
Make It clear
Little question
Wanna know just how you feel

If I said my heart was beating loud
If we could escape the crowd somehow
If I said I want your body now
Would you hold it against me

Cause you feel like paradise
I need a vacation tonight
So if I said I want your body now
Would you hold it against me

Hey You might think
That I'm crazy
But I know I'm just your type
I'mma be a little hazy
But you just cannot deny

There's a spark in between us
When we're dancing on the floor
I want more
Wanna see It
So I'm asking you tonight

If I said my heart was beating loud
If we could escape the crowd somehow
If I said I want your body now

Would you hold it against me

Cause you feel like paradise
I need a vacation tonight
So if I said I want your body now
Would you hold it against me

If I said I want your body
Would you Hold It Against Me?

(Yeah)

(Ah)

(Oh)

Gimme something good
Don't wanna wait I want It now (na-na-now)
Pop It like a hood
And show me how you work It out

(alright)
If I said my heart was beating loud
If I said I want your body now
Would you hold it against me

If I said my heart was beating loud
If we could escape the crowd somehow
If I said I want your body now
Would you hold it against me

Cause you feel like paradise
I need a vacation tonight
So if I said I want your body now
Would you hold it against me

According to the Marine that posted the video, Corporal Andrew Tarin, the motivation behind creating and posting the video was that they heard it on a bus ride to the Marine Corps Base and their "aim was to put out a video that would make our friends and families smile" ("Interview: Meet the Marines," 2011).

The video became viral very quickly, and many media outlets picked it up and covered it in their newscasts and online newspapers. Some parodies and video responses were generated on Youtube as well.

Although this video was, in relation to other military themed videos on Youtube "successful," it was hardly original. According to Clay Shirky in "Cognitive Surplus" "on the spectrum of creative work, the difference between the mediocre and the good is vast. Mediocrity is, however, still on the spectrum; you can move from mediocre to good in increments. The real gap is between doing nothing and doing something, and someone making [Internet meme] has bridged that gap…" (Shirky, 2010). Although Shirky was specifically speaking about the Internet meme known as "Lolcats," the military lip dub is similar in that it is generally a deployed/abroad military unit performing a lip-synched version of a popular song and sharing it on Youtube. These Marines were not the first to create a video of this type, and they probably aren't the last. Shirky might say "at least they were doing something," and that it was the sharing, not the making, that was the motivation for the Marines to create it and post it online. I believe the military lip dub Internet meme is an evolution of karaoke or a drag show with the creative effort akin to that of Lolcats.

Although it was hardly innovative in the spectrum of originality in user-generated or shared content, this particular video received a lot of attention, views and appreciation from viewers and that is the main motivation behind my exploring this phenomenon.

I believe the appeal for the views and "viral" sharing of the video lies in the viewer's recognition of the apparent liberation of these Marines expressing and laughing at themselves, despite the harsh conditions in which they live. In a nation where media outlets share endless "number of deaths" stories and updates, as one user put it, many people are desensitized and deluded by the dehumanization of Operation Enduring Freedom and what is left of Operation Iraqi Freedom. Another Youtube user commented on the video in reflection of guys dressing up as women and singing popular songs in previous wars, and the similarities to what these Marines are currently doing in the video.

"This is no different. In fact, it's better, because every time one of these videos is posted, people everywhere can see that in addition to being effective soldiers, these men and women are HUMAN. They have senses of humor and find fun in a situation that would break down a Joe Schmo. If I said you guy's rock, would you hold it against me?" (atarin18, 2011).

By utilizing Mikhail Bakhtins theory of Carnivalesque and other theories to improve upon it to analyze the video and user comments, I hope to discover the benefits and consequences/implications this military lip dub as form of Carnivalesque has on society.

Carnivalesque

Bakhtin's theory of Carnivalesque originates in his study on Rabelais and the Carnival as it existed in the pre-to mid-Renaissance period. According to Bakhtin in "Rabelais and his World," the Carnival culture externalized the joy of Europe's rebirth during this period. (Vanderbilt, 2011) Although Carnival and its forms today are tame in comparison to the culture that Bakhtin described during the Renaissance, the same ideas and traits he describes can be applied to modern Carnival.

Although Carnival is epitomized by leveling the playing field and the suspension of "temporary hierarchic distinctions and barriers among men…" (Vanderbilt, 2011), it is important to note that the realization of an alternative, Carnivalesque world is not synonymous with revolution, but a change from one world to another (Grindon, 2004). Therefore it is not "anarchic or irresponsible, but a diverse tactic that may be implemented and sustained wherever there is a dominant regime."

There are many themes of ambivalent laughter present in the video. The natural setting of the video is a Marine base in Afghanistan, yet the music indicates a club scene. The world around them is based on destruction, yet the video is creativity and expression. There is no alcohol, no loud music blaring and the Marines are not allowed to engage in sexual activity, yet the lyrics to the song are very provocative and sexual. Although the video is a variation of a parody on Britney Spears, the video isn't simply parodic. It is filled with irony, but it isn't simply ironic. It is a satire of pop music, but it isn't simply satirical. The laughter in the video has no object and it is ambivalent, meaning there are simultaneous and conflicting ideas at work (Lechte, 2007).

The video laughs at itself and those that create the oppression and turmoil it seeks to escape. It embraces lowness, especially the idea of debasement; lowering the value of certain hierarchies.. By debasing the people in it and the whole system present in it, it evens an often uneven playing field. In this video there is no leader or rank, in fact all hierarchies are suspended, a key element to the purpose of Carnival. It evenings many different groups; junior enlisted vs. senior enlisted, enlisted vs. officers, Marines and civilians, women and men. This temporary moment of liberation "involves the refusal of leaders, of sacrifice, of roles, freedom for everyone to realize himself." (Grindon, 2004) Most of the Marines in it receive equal time and attention.

The lyrics in the song also provide many instances of stark contrast and the ambivalence of laughter. The lyric "they're playing my favorite song" is the DJ playing certain music in the context of a nightclub, but in the context of Afghanistan they are witness and present in the middle of the sounds of war, artillery and ammunition. The lyric "you feel like paradise/and I need a vacation tonight." is interesting because the singer is witnessing paradise and a sense of vacation in someone she just met on a dance floor, but the Marines are singing it staring right into the camera, technology being their only access and escape into freedom and from the hot sandbox in which they live and work.

In addition to the ambivalent laughter of the scene, the Marines themselves help reveal and illuminate the "ambivalent, all-embracing logic of Carnival" (Lechte, 2007). They exist on many borders; including that of art and life, freedom and oppression and creativity and uniformity. The important thing to note is that the Marines masks help reveal the ambivalence of the Carnival because it is obviously distorting and "reveals and plays with contradiction" (Lechte, 2007). The "masks" I refer to aren't necessarily those of a clown or monster, but obvious ways the Marines cover up and transform.

One of the more apparent masks the Marines wear is clothing. Although they are in their uniforms, just as they would be any other day, in this video they come alive and play with the uniform -- as if it were Britney's outfit. A male Marine dances suggestively and unzips and peels away the top portion of his flight suit. A female Marine wears "boots and utes," that is, everything in her camouflage utility uniform except for her cover and blouse, sashaying around in a tight green undershirt revealing her curves and locking eyes with the camera. These uniforms change from the drab, military apparel meant to cover Marines and stifle their sexuality into form-fitting and revealing costumes that express them as sexual beings. Bakhtin explains the mask is connected with "gay relativity and the merry negation of uniformity and similarity."

In the video gender also becomes a mask. This is a phenomenon not only witnessed in this particular video, but other prominent military lip dubs feature soldiers over Lady Gaga and other hyper-feminine pop singers. Most of the Marines in the video are men, and the hyper masculinity of the Marines with the feminine voice and character in the song provide an interesting transformation. This mask of "metamorphosis and violation of natural boundaries" contains the playful element of life, compared to the serious nature of the military and its culture.

The masks these Marines wear are never serious, each one of them deals with the playfulness of life, including clothing and gender, but also masks of voice, creativity, expression, suppression of rank, freedom of thought and will, movement and provocative sexual dances, and race. According to Lechte "it is never serious unless we understand that to refuse to give seriousness absolute power is a serious matter. The exhortation of the Carnival is, as a result, that we should enter the game of life, masked: that is, ambivalently, irreverently, and with a spirit of laughter."

As the Marines laugh at those who oppress them, there is also laughter at themselves as subjects and objects of laughter. The Marines aren't the only participants in this video or in military lip dub as a form of Carnival, though.

Youtube as the venue for Carnival provides a way for a community to develop and people engage, interact and participate. According to Bakhtin, "Dialogism is a fundamental aspect of the Carnival -- a plurality of 'fully valid consciousnesses' each bringing with them a different point of view and way of seeing the world." In my analysis of the video, I found many different forms of dialogue among users, and users and between the Marines in the video (Vanderbilt, 2011).

Messages that were responses or comments to other users or the Marines were more common than any other type of comment I found. The conversation was very widely ranged, but the most significant amount of it was debating the freedom of expression service members should/shouldn't have while deployed. While there were a few that argued against it, many people took to defending the Marines and argue that they should have freedom of expression.

"This is amazing but they must be really bored over there to do this -- don't they have some military stuff to do?" asked "nickleneospots."

"@nickleneospots they usually do, but also they have their free time when things are quiet, its not always work work work work" said "leesvillehigh2015."

"@nickleneospots you are a flamming liberal. When we arent getting attacked and we have some FREE time form protecting your F****** Freedom to post ignorant a** s*** like that…then ya we do use our spare time to do something silly so we can stay sane because the next day we could be killed" said "brittinaylk."

Next a Marine that is in the video responded and joined the conversation, saying "That's what im talking about brother. We appreciate it. We are human and were just joking around. The Marines @work laughed for weeks about the video," said "rukbatluupa," (atarin18, 2011).

Dialogism is a very important aspect in the community of this military lip dub as form of Carnival. Although some criticized the video, some praised it and others requested more, Bakhtin argues that the input of those outside of a culture "opens new possibilities for each culture, reveals hidden potentials, promotes renewal and enrichment and creates new potentials, new voices that may become realizable in a future dialogic interaction" (Vanderbilt, 2011).

The back and forth exchanges of view points and criticism/praise doesn't hurt the form as Carnival, even the negative exchange offer a crucial element to the Carnival as practice. According to Bakhtin "The dual image combining praise and abuse seeks to grasp the very moment of this change, the transfer of the old to the new, from death to life" (Lechte, 2007).

Although it seems on the surface the viewers and users who comment on the video are merely outsiders looking in, they are in fact participating in the Carnival by interacting and engaging with the ideas. Even those commenters who negate or provide negative criticism are both actors and spectators at once, who laugh at the Marines and other users and are laughed at in return. It is this festival of laughter that is "one of the essential forms of truth concerning the world" (Lechte, 2007) and creates the ambivalence that sets Carnival up as a festival for reincarnation and change.

It is the combination of the ambivalence of laughter, the masks transforming and revealing/playing with contradictions and the participants of the military lip dub that make the form into a tradition of Carnival. By poking fun at the seriousness of the "officialdom," the military lip dub as Carnival sets itself up as a way to poke fun and point fingers and laughter toward those who seek to oppress it. Although this form is set up nicely as Carnival and it all seems to fit, perhaps Carnival as practice is less predictable at changing the rituals and laws of society.

Unintended Consequences/Implications of Military Lipdub as Carnival

Where the Renaissance Carnival Bakhtin describes is a temporary and "in the moment" kind of event, the video online exists as a world where actors/participants can visit and join in the festivities at any time. Thus, rather than a set number of actors/participants attending at a time set by someone else, which may have been true during the Renaissance, online timing is purely at the discretion of the people who are participating. On the surface, it seems this Carnival square is even more free and open to the masses. If the

Carnival of the Renaissance could be attended by hundreds of millions of people all at one time, would it make the changes Carnival indicates be even more rapid or powerful? Is this form liberating for those who seek the ambivalent laughter the Carnival provides, or is the online medium providing new ways people are trapped in hierarchical boundaries?

Despite the potential benefits the military lip dub poses as form of Carnival, this video shows how the form may in fact be giving more power to the hierarchy and dogmas the video is set to oppose.

According to Grindon, "Bakhtin argued that in medieval period official culture, with its seriousness allied to power and authority, was too strong for medieval man to resist it. Against the ideological and physical force of the medieval state, Carnivals "consciousness of freedom…could only be limited and utopian." This may indicate that because our society is so integrated in capitalism, Carnival may not be as strong. Are the Marines and viewers exhibiting and living a liberated or conscious sense of freedom, or is their thought process and creative expression in this form limited by the medium capitalism points them to?

The name Youtube implies that this is a channel of "you," not advertisers or news outlets or television agencies but the regular folks expressing themselves and creating a community of sharing and collaborating from the ground up, which sounds like exactly the right kind of space to host a Carnival. But in its reality, Youtube exists under the same social conditions of any capitalist production; it is owned by Google and is a for-profit company.

If capitalism does in fact point us toward itself for a venue for expression, Youtube as the manifestation of it in this particular example, it doesn't mean that because the Carnival is held on its grounds the form can't exist as a place of temporary liberation. It isn't the act of being on Youtube that violates Carnival and its potential; it's the act of being on Youtube because it's the only way the limited conscious of the people can think to be. In Bakhtin's Carnival, during the Renaissance the people were the Carnival and officialdom was subject to its rituals and laws. In the military lip dub as Carnival, capitalism has subjected the people to its rituals and laws of expression, and the form as it relates to democracy is going backwards, despite its initial liberating feeling. In this example, the potency or potential of Carnival is turned on its head as capitalism uses it in its favor.

The potency of the military lip dub as Carnival is also decreased by the separation of participants and spectators. Those who exist within the Carnival, the Marines and users, revel in the festival of laughter and the hilarity that is directed toward everyone. The spectators, however, are not only watching from an outside viewpoint but they are sitting behind a machine and from any number of locations. The festival of laughter works when the community is together and engaged, but if someone doesn't have the time to sit and watch a three minute video and only watches a piece, or only sees a video clip on the news the hilarity can't be lived or experienced. Bakhtin specifies that Carnival is not a spectacle to be observed, it is the hilarity lived by everyone.

Not only the military lip dub, but the Internet meme or communication on Youtube in general is a huge indicator of the negative effects of capitalism on the freedom of expression. Rather than oppose forms of communication people adapt to those that are presented to them, and this Internet meme is as much a creative endeavor as a Lolcat. It is taking someone else's idea, changing it slightly and sending it into the universe as an act of "sharing." Some Internet memes become hugely popular, with ungodly amounts of people "creating" one too. Although the life spans of these Internet memes are short, they may not be a starting point for other people to move on to bigger and better things. Instead of changing, things rearrange. New Internet memes are born and die, and people are trapped in their cycle without escaping and relying on pure creativity to do something new and unique.

Even though capitalism has control of people's communication and venues for expression, the military lip dub as form isn't necessarily working against capitalism. I can't argue that these Marines or people participate in military lip dubs as Carnival in order to oppose capitalism itself, but merely some of the entities that operate under its protective umbrella. These being most specifically the media and the military. Although capitalism has proven its control over the consciousness of freedom, the media and the military have done the same but by different, more specific mechanisms.

One of Bakhtin's arguments in his theory of Carnivalesque is the notion of artifice, or that the roles the actors play in turn play them. The Marines role in the video, not the masks they wear, are as Youtube stars. They play liberated, free, creative and financially unmotivated entertainers on Youtube, in the form of the military lip dub. Carnival discourages us from looking under their masks to see who the Marines REALLY are, but as an accumulation of the roles they play and are in turn played back (UVM, 2011). One of the appeals to people watching the video, as indicated frequently in user comments, is the fact that on television, the media pretty much only portray Marines and soldiers in general as nameless drones fighting a war in the distance, or as casualties. One user commented "It's cool to see something besides number of deaths."

In this video, the dehumanization of the war by the media is opposed by the Marines being silly and human. That's what people like about it, and they like that even though they hear constant reports of death and war-related mental illness, there is some hope. These Marines challenge the common rhetoric of war deaths in the media with proof of life in this Carnival form.

This sounds positive, but the roles the Marines play turn around and play them, labeling them as Youtube stars and spreading their faces across the Internet and television on many news sites. The Marines became Youtube stars overnight, and acted as such. The media regained control of how our military are represented, it's still up to them and what they think will get them the most money, not what is truly important. One quick Google search for "Marines-Britney Spears" and the top results show interviews with the Marines and commentary on the video on Fox News, CNN, USA Today and the Huffington Post. On the next pages CBS News, MSNBC, LA Times and Dailymail all have their headlines.

In the beginning, the video was a socially relevant form of Carnival challenging the media and what people want/deserve to know about our troops overseas. But, after 3 million views and the public support by a capitalist-owned pop star, the media took notice and got a piece of the pie. If the people want to see these Marines alive and joyous, the media wants some of that popularity as news. Suddenly, the importance of the struggle these Marines represented in the form between life and death and the troops portrayal on the media was relegated to a spectacle, something controlled by officialdom and subject to its rituals and laws. Once again, the media controls portrayal of the war. Grindon says that some argue that "Carnival is a social safety valve that allows the official world to operate unhindered the rest of the time, and is in this sense complicit with that which it superficially opposes" (Grindon, 2004). Although the media did pick it up and probably caused it to be viewed a lot more than if it had been left to be discovered and shared among the community of the people, the higher numbers don't indicate more potential for this form as Carnival for change and reincarnation. A video spread and shared among the community, the viewers and Marines as actors and spectators simultaneously, has value in that the power is in the hands of the people who appreciate it. They celebrate the ambivalent laughter, the themes of life vs. death and joy vs. a metaphorical prison of silence. As soon as the media picked it up the military lip dub as form is damaged and imprisoned. Just as capitalism gained control over the video, the media gained control over it as well therefore killing the form as Carnival and destroying the change and reincarnation it could have caused.

As the military lip dub as form is now proven to be a "social safety valve" for capitalism and media, the "officialdom," I will look at how the military has found a way to use the lip dub in form as a social safety valve as well.

The military, and the government in general, are often characterized by a struggle between transparency and secrecy, especially during times of war. For a long time, social media was discouraged and often banned to service members in combat zones. According to the U.S. Department of Defense, in February 2010 military members were allowed to access Web 2.0 platforms from non-classified government computers, under the stipulations they don't compromise operational security or engage in prohibited activities or visit prohibited Web sites. Deputy Defense Secretary William J. Lynn III, who signed the policy, said it "strikes a critical balance between the benefits and potential vulnerabilities" of the applications (Miles, 2010).

Despite the authorization and downright encouragement for service members to utilize social media to "stay in contact with their loved ones," the social conditions of rank and hierarchy lend the military to less encouragement for creativity and expression. I will now explain what is the likely evolution for service members in motivation for developing and sharing the military lip dub as form for Carnival.

Most of the Marines in the video are junior enlisted Marines, and the one who created and shared it is an E-4. I spent four years as a junior enlisted Marines, two of them as an E-4. This particular culture of Marines is diverse, but as many learn and are conditioned for in boot camp, there is very little room to speak out against someone higher ranking or to voice opinions at all. The most important job junior enlisted Marines can do is listen to their superiors, and not disobey or argue a direct order. There are avenues for bypassing certain orders or decisions made by someone superior to them, but the "appropriate" action of "requesting mast" in order to speak to a more senior member of the command requires paperwork and difficult routes of communication, so it is made difficult for them.

This freezing of communication to those above them is only made worse by the lack of communication they have with family members while deployed. Although advancements have been made in communication by email and other social networking, compared to other wars, at the same time they are "on the job" more hours than they would be at home, and the kind of information they can share is limited. The stress and anxiety that goes with being deployed is hard to communicate to someone who isn't there, and worrying about whether or not they will see them again isn't particularly conducive to relaxation.

Communication barriers with superiors "officialdom" and the information that is being passed to their loved ones via the media "officialdom," may be part of the reason why the Marines expressed their voices through the Carnivalesque military lip dub. The suppression of their voices and their ability to communicate feelings and anxiety is expressed in the video. In it, they get to be someone else, they get to be Britney Spears; a pop star who is viewed by many as a symbol of freedom, sexuality, and liberation. They wear the mask of Britney and her voice moves through their lips. She is so much the opposite of these troops that the mask is obviously distorting.

These Marines are able to laugh at themselves and laugh at their own imprisonment, the military allows them so little freedom of expression and creativity that their suppression manifests itself in a joyous act of Carnival. A glimpse "of a world turned upside down, a topsy-turvy universe free of toil, suffering and inequality. Carnival celebrates temporary liberation from the prevailing truth and established order; it marks the suspension of all hierarchical rank, privileges, norms and prohibitions (Grindon, 2004).

In this video, the Marines are no longer young Lance Corporals separated from their families and trapped in a world where they have no voice, but they are Britney Spears, the woman whose voice and identity transcend cultures and earthly borders. The military lip dub as form of Carnival allows service members to express themselves in a way they can laugh at themselves and those rules and limitations the "officialdom" sets upon them, which is liberating. A lip dub may not be the biggest creative endeavor, but they are communicating and expressing themselves in a way others have shown they can, which is indicated by the popularity of troops creating very similar videos like these on the Internet. There is safety in the lack of individuality of the lip dub, because in the military they do not want to stick out as wild, but there is also room for them to be "heard" without worry of penalization.

However liberating this seems and probably feels to them, it is still adapting to the restrictive forms of communication the "officialdom" sets upon them, instead of opposing them. In fact, not only are they adapting to the restrictions the military sets upon their communication mediums, they are adapting to the restrictions the lip dub genre sets upon them. They have so many sets of restrictions set upon them that their attempt at Carnival has, in turn, been smothered and beaten into the ground. This is the opposite of free will, liberation and democracy.

The military benefits from these military lip dubs as form, because they have the control and the service members are bending to the rituals and laws the service sets upon them and not the other way around, as Carnival is meant to be. A form that is used by service members to express themselves in spite of the military rules they are subject to is only hurt when they give the military even more control to dictate how they can or can't communicate and express themselves.

In conclusion, despite the many traits military lip dub as form of Carnival has in accordance with Bakhtins theory of Carnivalesque, there are certain flaws to the execution and medium it is expressed in that create even more boundaries and hierarchy/control problems than before. The traits of the Carnival: ambivalent laughter, the actors/spectators as subjects and objects of laughter, the Carnival figures that exist on borders of art and life, and the masks which reveal the logic of Carnival all create a foundation upon which Carnival can be potent and catalyst for change, by enforcing rituals and laws in opposition to "officialdom." It is the execution of this Carnival, in a society where people are trapped by capitalism into specific ways of expressing themselves and communicating where the main problem arises. No matter how the military lip dub creates a seemingly new form of liberation and seems to carry the power, the struggle is always won by the officialdom, be it capitalism, the media or the military. The people in this military lip dub Carnival, whether they are laughing at themselves and directing the laughter at those who control them, are so subject to the rituals and laws of the various hierarchies that their expression isn't expression at all, their free will is a farce and most unfortunately, the democracy they fight for gives them no freedom at all. And they don't even realize it.

Conclusion

My research and analysis contributes to the field of research being done on Internet memes and Youtube. It also contributes to the understanding of how people feel creative and expressive on the Internet, and how companies might use that knowledge to make money or connect with them. It also contributes to our understanding of how society tries to cope with war in the Internet age.

There are several main points I would like readers to take from my research. One point is that no matter how free we think our expression is, the act of creating and sharing on Youtube might actually be limiting our freedom in ways we cannot imagine. The military lip dub as an act of Carnival has the potential to help people escape from several entities that attempt to control how the war is portrayed and what we get to view, but by utilizing Capitalist driven mediums of expression like Youtube, it ends up limiting the freedom of deployed service members and the American public because it is used as a safety valve by the media and government.

One of the strengths to my method was that I was able to research and find meaning in the short amount of time I had. An Internet meme has a short lifespan, so in order to point out the significance of this phenomenon one will need to be able to find results in less time while the subject is still relevant. One of the limitations is the amount of time I had to gather data and observe/code. As a summer research paper, I had about three months from the proposal of my professor to a draft. Future research might include observing the behavior and social patterns that emerge on other military lip dub videos.

References

atarin18. (2011). Hold it Against Me 266 Rein Marines Official Version. *Youtube*. Retrieved May 28, 2011 from http://www.youtube.com/watch?v=rCrG6TzG-nw

Burgess, J. , & Green, J. (2009). *YouTube: Online Video and Participatory Culture* (p. 172). Polity. Retrieved from http://www.amazon.com/dp/0745644791

Burgess, Jean (2008) *'All Your Chocolate Rain Are Belong to Us?' Viral Video, YouTube and the Dynamics of Participatory Culture*. In: UNSPECIFIED, (ed) Video Vortex Reader: Responses to YouTube. Institute of Network Cultures, Amsterdam, pp. 101-109.

Grindon, Gavin. (2004). Carnival Against Capital: A Comparison of Bakhtin, Vaneigem and Bey. Anarchist Studies 12:2, 147-161. Retrieved July 12, 2011 from http://kingston.academia.edu/GavinGrindon/Papers/170606/Carnival_Against_Capital_A_Comparison_of_Bakhtin_Vaneigem_and_Bey

Hanuman, A.R.N. Dr. (2011). *Hope and Despair: A Carnivalesque Study of Kurt Vonnegut's Cat's Cradle*. The Criterion: An International Journal in English. Retrieved July 1, 2011 from http://www.the-criterion.com/V2/n1/Alapati.pdf

Interview: Meet the Marines Behind the Britney Spears Viral Video. (2011). *Military Times*. Retrieved May 27, 2011 from http://militarytimes.com/blogs/battle-rattle/2011/04/27/interview-meet-the-marines-behind-the-britney-spears-viral-video/

Lange, P. G. (2007), Publicly Private and Privately Public: Social Networking on YouTube. Journal of Computer-Mediated Communication, 13: 361–380. doi: 10.1111/j.1083-6101.2007.00400.x http://www.cs.uwaterloo.ca/~apidduck/CS432/Assignments/YouTube.pdf

Lechte, John. (2007). *Fifty Key Contemporary Thinkers*. Taylor & Francis.

Mikhail Bakhtin. *Vanderbilt University*. Retrieved June 21, 2011 from http://www.vanderbilt.edu/AnS/Anthro/Anth206/mikhail_bakhtin.htm

Miles, Donna. (2010). New Policy Authorizes Social Media Access, With Caveats. *U.S. Department Of Defense.* Retrieved July 6, 2011 from http://www.defense.gov/news/newsarticle.aspx?id=58117

Shirky, Clay. (2010). *Cognitive Surplus: Creativity and Generosity in a Connected Age.* Penguin.

The Carnival Model. *University of Wisconsin-Milwaukee.* Retrieved July 5, 2011 from https://pantherfile.uwm.edu/wash/www/102_18.htm

The Internet Meme: A Joyous Thing of Laughter. (2011). *New Media Research Studio.* Retrieved June 28, 2011 from http://cultureandcommunication.org/tdm/nmrs/sp1/2011/04/24/the-internet-meme-a-joyous-thing-of-laughter/

ABOUT THE AUTHORS

The authors were all students at Texas Lutheran University in Fall 2011 or the semesters leading up to "Living Privately in Public: Social Media and Responsibility." Most of them graduated either in December 2011 or May 2012. **Brandon Boylan** and **Aubrey Buzek** wrote their papers for a special seminar on social media during the summer of 2011. **Elizabeth Beck-Dietert** and **Courtney Tarrillion** began their projects in a special topics class on social media in the fall semester 2011. Tarrillion completed her project in for her senior seminar in communication studies. Like the communication papers, the psychology studies usually began as a class projects, primarily in social psychology and human sexuality. However, the courses in social psychology and human sexuality were not directed at the theme of the Krost Symposium but instead, the research fortuitously lined up with the 2011 topic. The psychology students pursued their research independently, rather than in senior seminars. All of the authors of the psychology papers – **Melissa Fike, Nathan J. Fry, , Zoila Garcia, Joshua A. Haby, Caleb Hoffmann, Canaan A. Hoffmann, Catherine R. Hoffmann, Kyle A. Leihsing, Amber Mellon,and Andrew B. Serafino** – have presented their individual studies as posters at the Southwestern Psychological Association Conferences in 2010, 2011 and 2012. While the authors of the communication papers all majored in communication studies, students with majors in art and music worked alongside their peers with majors in psychology to complete these studies.